MORE THAN A RING

Don Beebe's unlikely path to the NFL and a Super Bowl Championship

by

Don Beebe

with
Bob Schaller

Foreword by Reggie White

Introduction by Brett Favre

Extra Point by Marv Levy

Angel Press of WI   Neshkoro, Wisconsin

est. 1986

Angel Press of WI
PO Box 48
Neshkoro, WI 54960

Copyright 1998 by Don Beebe
ISBN: 0-939995-29-8

Library of Congress Number: 97-078224

Angel Press of WI
PO Box 643
Wautoma, WI 54982

Front cover photographs by
Vern Biever, Mike Groll, and Torry Names

Back cover photograph by Mike Groll

Publisher......................................J. H. Schlaefer
Editor..Larry Names

Printed in USA

Table of Contents

To my

sister Beth and brother-in-law Paul,
sister Diane and brother-in-law Bob,
brother Dan and sister-in-law Stacy,
and brother Dave and sister-in-law Mandy,

you are simply the best. The reason we are so close is we love Jesus Christ. No wonder we want to live back home. We can't imagine our life living away from all of you. You are the best sisters and brothers a person could ever ask for.

To

Mom and Dad

what can I say but that I could write a book on the two of you. You have shown your five kids what it is like to raise a family putting Jesus Christ first. Even though all marriages have their ups and downs, you leaned on God through the tough times and stuck it out, especially in a day and age where families are consistently falling apart.

To my beautiful wife,

Diana,

the most important person that God has put into my life. You are my best friend and you always seem to pick me up when I am down. You have given me the greatest joy in having our three children: Amanda, Chad and MaKayla. I am truly a blessed man. I love you more now than I did ten years ago when we were married, and I can't imagine what I'll feel like ten years form now. I look forward to spending the rest of my life with you.

Lastly, I would like to thank
the most important Person in my life, my Lord and Savior,
Jesus Christ.
Without You, I am nothing, but with You, I am everything. You
have blessed me with a great family and a great career, and I can't
wait until we shall meet face to face.

I love you all.

ACKNOWLEDGMENTS

First, I'd like to thank Bob Schaller for helping me write this book. He took no compensation and let all his proceeds go toward Chadron State College, too. May the Lord richly bless you, Bob, for your thoughts have not gone unnoticed.

To Bob and Lynn LaMonte, this project could not have worked without your help. Thanks for putting this thing all together. You two are very special.

To Larry Names, my editor at Angel Press, thanks to you and Angel Press for publishing my book. Larry, you put in long hours to see this project through. I am extremely grateful.

To Bruce Craddock's family, he was a big influence on me. I will always remember Coach Craddock.

To Frank Reich, Jim Kelly, Steve Tasker, Nick Nicolau, Reggie White, Brett Favre, Marv Levy, Mike Holmgren, Brad Smith, Bill Polian, John Butler, Scott Berchtold, Con

Marshall, Bill O'Boyle, Todd Auer, and Dick Schaap for being interviewed for the book. It's greatly appreciated and your friendships mean a lot to me.

Lastly, Diana and I have been blessed with so many close friends. You all will forever hold a special place in our hearts because friends are friends forever when the Lord is the Lord of them.

God bless and thank you.

FOREWORD

by

Reggie White

Jhad already heard a lot about Don's Christian walk before we became teammates in 1996 with the Green Bay Packers. He was up against so many obstacles along the way. People hear his story, and it is so encouraging.

Don is not the kind of person to present himself any different than what he is. It is kind of hard to find guys like that. He is very sincere. After we won the Super Bowl last season, I promised my wife that I would not add anything to my schedule. But one of Don's friends was killed by a drunk driver back where Don was raised in Illinois. The man's wife had two little children to take care of. Don called and wanted to do something special to help them.

I had to be a part of that. What Don did by having the football camp to raise money for that family was special.

Don really came through for us last season (in 1996). He

makes the most of his gifts. We preach the same message from the Lord. When I speak to people, I compare a landscaping project to society. That is, to landscape, you take all these flowers of different colors, different breeds of plants and put them all together. And it just makes the most beautiful picture.

Now we, as a society, are made up of different colors and ethnic groups, and the picture needs to be seen as beautiful. Look at Don Beebe and me; we couldn't be more different in appearance. I'm a large, black man, and Don is smaller and white. But we are no different. We love each other. Sure, our cultures our different, but our Kingdom is the same. I am proud to have Don as one of my brothers.

INTRODUCTION

by

Brett Favre

We would not have won the Super Bowl last year without Don Beebe.

Of course, we had a lot of guys step up all season, but you have to mention Don as soon as you mention anyone else.

We lost two receivers, Robert Brooks and Antonio Freeman, and Don just comes in during a Monday night game against San Francisco and catches more passes (11) for more yards (220) than anyone has in a long time (12 years), or anyone will again for the Green Bay Packers. His perspective is so good, that in a way it's not surprising he always seems to be one of the players who steps forward for the big games, or picks up a team when the chips are down.

Don, or "Beebs," his nickname, is a good friend. He gets along with everyone, which helped him fit in quickly when he got here. He's such a good person that it almost gets overlooked what a good football player he really is. He hustles, which everyone knows about from watching him in the Super Bowl. He's fast—he's our fastest receiver in Green Bay, and we have some fast ones. He knows how to run good routes, and he has really good hands. Of course, he knows how to get open, which is very important.

He's really a unique player because he can do so many things. He can return kicks, and he's so fast that he's a weapon in a lot of ways.

All the receivers here had several years in this system, so Don, when he got here before the 1996 season, had the most to learn in the shortest amount of time. But he's very smart, and he worked hard to make the adjustment.

Our friendship means a lot to me. We play golf a lot. Although half the time I ask him to play golf, he can't because he's doing something with his wife, Diana, or with his kids. That doesn't bother me, because he's such a great family man, such a great role model. Anyone who knows Don Beebe knows he'll never put anything ahead of his family.

At the same time, he's always helped me out when I needed something. Actually, he's been there every time I've needed him to be, if I need something signed, or something like that.

Everyone who knows Don Beebe's name knows he's a deeply Christian man. The way he handles that makes him special. On the one hand, he's not afraid to talk about it to anyone, and he speaks to a lot of groups about his faith. On the other hand, he knows when not to push it, because that can turn someone off. Guys in the locker room aren't afraid to be themselves around Don, although everyone has a lot of respect for him. That's really a good quality. Because not all Christians are that way. They have to push, push, push every second and that ends up turning some people off.

Don just wants people to know that Christianity is there for them. The way he handles it makes people respect him even more.

Beebe and the Lombardi Trophy at the press conference after Super Bowl XXXI. "I sure waited a long time for that moment."

MORE THAN A RING

Beebe walks off the field with a Super Bowl victory, carrying his son Chad. To the left is Beebe's younger brother Dan Beebe.

1

ANOTHER TITLE FOR TITLETOWN

The NFL's Most Valuable Player, Brett Favre, took the snap, and then took a knee.

The Superdome noise hit frightening decibel levels as Green Bay wide receiver Don Beebe approached Favre from behind. Green Bay had just pounded New England, 35-21, in the Super Bowl on January 26, 1997. Favre stood up with the football and smiled as Don arrived in front of him.

"Can I have the game ball?" Don asked Favre. "I'd like to give it to my family."

"You bet," Favre told Don. "You deserve it."

Favre flipped the ball to Don, who ran toward the stands, waving the ball.

"That was so nice of Brett to do that," Don said. "Here he is, the league's most valuable player, and he lets me have the game ball. He never said a word about it—we've never talked about it since he tossed it to me."

Favre says he wanted Beebe to have the ball.

"I just thought it was perfect," Favre said. "Here's a guy who was on a team that lost four Super Bowls, a guy who had a couple of bad injuries. But he came back every time, and was always the perfect team player and the perfect man off the field. He deserved that game ball. I was glad to give it to him."

After coming out the loser four times in the Super Bowl as a member of the Buffalo Bills, Don had earned his Super Bowl ring.

But it was more than a ring.

"God has blessed me," Don said. "And being a part of the Super Bowl champion is another opportunity to get the word out."

Beebe went over to the sidelines, and shared the moment with his family. Diana, the couple's two oldest children, Amanda and Chad, and Don's younger brother, Dan, came down to the field.

"That," Don said, "was quite a special moment."

The Packers' season highlight film ends with Don and his wife, Diana, on the field sharing a hug that never seems to end. Beebe was in the end zone with a Super Bowl championship. But to a man like Don, whose life is dedicated to spreading his faith, it was more than a ring.

Yet nearly a year earlier, in February of 1996, when Don was cut by the Carolina Panthers, the team he and the

Packers would end up defeating to earn the trip to the Super Bowl, Don knew he wanted to go to Green Bay. And while he couldn't imagine the satisfaction the Super Bowl win would bring, he had no doubt that he and the Packers would be in New Orleans on January 26, 1997, as world champions.

"I never doubted that we'd go to the Super Bowl and win," Don said. "I mean, that's how I knew it would be. Of course, when we got the home field for the playoffs and got to stay at Lambeau Field until the Super Bowl, it was just a matter of time."

After playing a key role during the regular season, Don didn't catch a pass in the Super Bowl. Still, he was ecstatic to see his teammates, Antonio Freeman, Andre Rison, and Desmond Howard, the game's MVP, find the end zone.

"I'd like to score a touchdown in a Super Bowl that we won," said Don, who had two touchdowns in losing Super Bowl performances with Buffalo. "But going into Super Bowl XXXI, I was talking to Antonio, Andre, and Desmond, and I said, 'I hope you get to score in the Super Bowl, it's great.' And all three got to taste that. It ended up being a victory, too, and that makes it more special."

In the weeks leading up to the Super Bowl, Don and more than a dozen Christian teammates for Green Bay, including Reggie White, Eugene Robinson, and Keith Jackson met for their weekly Bible study.

"I used the time leading up to the Super Bowl to share my faith," Don said. "We had our usual big group for a Bible study here in Green Bay just before we left for New Orleans. I told the guys that the hype is going to be unbelievable. So instead of wearing hats to promote candy bars or shoe companies, let's wear hats or shirts to promote your favorite Bible verse or hats that say, 'Jesus is Lord.' It was a good opportunity to spread the word. We did, and that made this experience mean even more."

Spreading the word is what Beebe has done through every stop of his wonderfully nonsensical trip to the NFL and five Super Bowls. Recruited by only one college, Don attended four colleges over the course of six years before finishing what would be his second, and final, year of college football. That final year was at Chadron State College in northwestern Nebraska, where Don played one year, after playing one year at Western Illinois. But he impressed scouts enough with his speed that the Bills were willing to make Don their top draft pick, the 82nd selection overall, in the 1989 Draft.

ABC sportscaster Dick Schaap wrote a book, *Return to Glory*, about the Packers 1996 Super Bowl season.

"Don is one of the great stories in sports," Schaap said. "He came from nowhere to play in five Super Bowls."

Don says he plans to finish his career in Green Bay. Teammate Derrick Mayes, also a wide receiver with Green Bay, said Beebe will leave the league the way he came into it.

"Don is still the fastest guy out here," Mayes said. "He does what's right. He has a lot of wisdom, and we all have a lot of respect for him."

With the ecstasy of a much-awaited Super Bowl crown came agony. Celebrating with Diana on a cruise to St.

Martin in the Virgin Islands, Don got an emergency call on the ship on February 25. It was his mother with news that one of his best friends from back home in Illinois, Jeff Still, had been killed by a drunk driver.

Don had brought Jeff to the Super Bowl in New Orleans. However, when Jeff came to New Orleans, he did not have a ticket. Don had already given out all of his allotment, but Jeff was still glad just to be there. At the last minute, Don's parents couldn't make the game and Jeff went. Through what followed with Jeff's death, Don said it was all the work of God.

"It was tough," Don said. "Jeff had accepted Christ six months before he passed away. He was just on fire for God. His wife, June, saw the change in Jeff's life. Standing over Jeff's body, June asked the pastor, 'Will I ever see Jeff again?' He said, 'There's only one way because Jeff's in heaven.' She said, 'How do I get to heaven?' The pastor told her that the only way was to accept Jesus Christ as her personal savior.

"You look at a tragedy like that and can't understand how that happens," Don said. "But if that never happens, June may never accept Christ, and that's a greater tragedy. This human life is such a short time on eternity's scale. Now, Jeff and June will spend eternity together. This funeral was a celebration. There was weeping and sorrow, but people left there touched. Everyone who spoke on Jeff's behalf talked about having a relationship with Christ. It was a touching, touching moment. It affected a lot of people's lives. Through Jeff's death, not just June, but several people I know of, and a couple more I have since heard about, came to know Christ."

Don's thoughts turned to Jeff's wife and the couple's two young boys, two-year-old Jake and two-month-old Jarred.

"It was devastating. On the plane ride home from the cruise, the Lord was pressing upon me to do something for the kids," Don said. "Initially, I thought about having a benefit golf tournament to raise money for them. But Jeff was about football, not golf, so I decided to put together a football camp. There wasn't anyone who didn't want to be a part of it. Reggie White was the first person I thought of. He was Jeff's favorite player, and Jeff played defensive line when he played, so that was good. Reggie said yes. Jim Kelly, he wanted to be there, but he had commitments. Still, he said he'd find a way, and he did. He literally came to the camp between flights and gave us all the time we needed. I called Desmond Howard, who had just signed with the Raiders after he was named the MVP of the Super Bowl for us. I only called three guys, and all three showed up."

The event raised $24,000 for the two boys' college fund.

Don's journey is a long, unpredictable one. However, he knows that God was with him through every unlikely step.

"How could you explain where I have been to, and where I am, without seeing the hand prints of the Lord all over this?" Don asks with a smile. "The path was never clear, never obvious and didn't always make sense at first. But He took me here and there because it was His plan. I have been blessed."

Jeff Still, Beebe's childhood friend and brother in Christ. Jeff's life was taken tragically by a drunken driver. "We miss you Jeff, but we have the comfort in knowing that you're with our Creator."

Great friends pulling together for the Jeff Still Camp of Dreams. Left to right: Desmond Howard, Jim Still, Mike Walker, Beebe, and Jim Kelly.

Don Beebe, Dave Beebe, and Dan Beebe with Jeff Still and Jim Still.

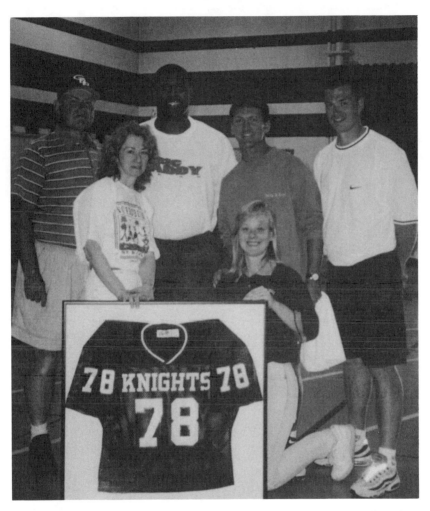

Jeff Still's high school football jersey was presented to his family at the Camp of Dreams, June 12, 1997. Left to right: Gary Still (Jeff's father), Reggie White, June Still (Jeff's wife), Beebe, and Jim Still (Jeff's brother).

2

THE FIRE INSIDE

David Beebe, Don's little brother, said the family has adapted to Don's competitiveness over the years. However, the process hasn't always been painless or easy.

"The thing you have to realize when you compete against Don is that he's not going to be happy until he wins," Dave said. "And then you need to realize that *you* won't be happy until he wins. He was absolutely miserable, unless he won."

Don concedes the point.

"The sad thing is, that's the truth," he said. "At times, I question whether I'm too competitive. I am so competitive, to a fault. I think it offends people sometimes. But I'm here today because of this fact. If I'm playing my mom in chess, I'm going to win. And then I'll tell her I love her. I don't care what it is, I'm going to win."

He has a hard time accepting losing.

"I don't know if I pout when I lose," Don said. "But I might say the other person had to cheat to win."

His brother Dan, three years younger than Don, said Don gets even more creative than that. "He won't actually cheat, but he'll change the rules, in the middle of a game even. He'll just invent rules. You'll be playing to 10 in basketball, and win 10-9. Don will say, 'You need to win by two.' Or, he'll invent a rule that anyone within one point of losing—if it's him—gets the ball, or something. Anything to give himself a chance to win."

The family fishing derby each year in Remer, Minnesota, might as well have been an event in the extreme games—because Don could not enjoy the rest of vacation if he didn't win. The family would put dots on a board in the cabin to mark who was ahead. Trailing, 12-year-old Don could not take it.

"Everyone else is spending time together, just sitting around and enjoying vacation," says little brother Dan. "But not Don. He takes five hours to fish because he couldn't wait until the next day to be in the lead."

"I was bound and determined to win," Don said. "I went out on the dock, used hot dogs and cheese as bait, and caught 118 bluegills."

His father was not about to spend the rest of the afternoon sticking dots on the board.

"I'm not putting 118 dots on the board," his father said, choosing instead to put one big blue dot on the board and writing "118 bluegills" on it.

"I couldn't believe that," Don said. "I caught 118 fish. I

should've gotten 118 dots on the board."

Shifting the competitiveness off is hard.

"I just hate to lose, refuse to lose," Don said. "I don't care what I'm doing. I can't let people pass me when I'm driving. It's a fault."

Ever since he was little, Don had energy to burn. While he was never in any real trouble, he did earn, by far, the most number of spankings from his father.

One of his more serious infractions came in, of all places, church. Seven-years-old at the time, Don was flipping spit-wads with a friend, one of which ended up hitting the pastor, who was praying at the time.

"The pastor said, 'Will the parents of the boys who are flicking spit-wads please come up and get their kids?' I felt this big grip on the back of my head pulling me up. It was Dad. He said, 'Son, we'll deal with this when we get home.' I've never been so scared on the way home."

"We were all scared for Don that day," said his oldest sister, Beth. "But he was in trouble every Sunday. My Dad would take us to his room if he had to spank us, and he rarely had to do that with any of us—except Don. It got to the point where when we'd get home from church, Don would just head up to Dad's room, whether he was told to or not, out of habit."

Don, who has two older sisters, Beth and Diane, and two younger brothers, Dan and David, admits as much. "It was like that every Sunday, to tell you the truth," he said. "I was just a go-go-go, nonstop kid. I never did anything that hurt anyone. I was just a nonstop kid, always doing things. I wasn't a kid who smoked or drank, and I never did steal or anything like that. But I was always mischievous. I had a lot of fun."

Diana, Don's wife, said her husband has learned to tone it down. The arrival of Amanda (April 16, 1991; then Chad, June 1, 1994; and MaKayla, November 8, 1996) helped. "He's gotten a lot better about it," she says. "Having three kids has made him mellow. But when I first started dating him, it was hysterical. I was like, 'Is there anything you don't compete in?'"

When Amanda was born, Don was still unable to get along without his daily fix of competition. The two would sit and watch *Jeopardy!*, with Don playing each round like it was a Super Bowl.

"It got to the point where Amanda would get involved," Diana said. "She used to hear the music to the show, come out in her walker, and she'd stare at the TV until the show was over."

Don was also stubborn.

During a family vacation on a lake in Autrain, Michigan, Don, 13 at the time, went out in a rowboat in a small bay, one that led to a much bigger lake. Don started to pass through two sand bars, but put down the anchor so he would not drift out to the lake. As the wind came up, Don started to row back in.

"But he wasn't going anywhere," said his father, who watching. "He had the anchor down."

Don rowed and rowed, and the boat didn't budge. The winds were getting stronger and stronger.

"I went out and told him to pull the anchor up and row

in," his father said.

"He must've told me to pull up anchor a thousand times," Don said. "He wasn't even 30 feet away from me, so I could hear him."

So why leave the anchor out?

"I was afraid if I pulled up the anchor, I'd get blown out into the lake and I'd die," Don said. "I really believed that I would die."

His father saw the fear, but knew Don could reach a resolution to the situation without his father's help. "He rowed for maybe 20 minutes, it seemed like. Aside from the fact he was scared, it would have been funny."

Finally, an exhausted Don was forced to quit rowing.

"I stopped and thought the wind would take me out to the big lake," Don said. "But it didn't."

So Don pulled the anchor in, and he still didn't drift out. Instead, he rowed easily back in, and pulled the boat to the dock.

"He went right past me, didn't say a word," his father said, noting that his son had to learn a lesson.

"I didn't get over that for a long time," Don said. "That was an important lesson—fear, basically—just that I had to trust that my dad would do what's best for me. My dad's the wisest man I ever met."

But Don did try to get even with his father, for years and years to come. One of those times came when Don was 19.

On Halloween night, he decided he finally had the perfect plan to scare his father.

"Scott Pierce (a brother-in-law) and I snuck into the

house through a back bedroom window. We made sure no one saw us as we went down to the basement and cut the lights to the house," Don said. "It was pitch black, and we could hear everyone upstairs."

That wasn't the end of the act.

"We had chains and were banging them against the wall," Don said.

Don's mother was scared.

"We called the police," Barb Beebe said. "We just didn't know what was going on."

The guys kept the act up. Finally, Don's father heard enough, and went marching downstairs to check the fuse box and get the lights back on.

"I waited for him, still as can be, and when he got in front of me I grabbed him around the neck and mouth and said in a tough voice, 'Don't try anything, or you'll get it,' trying to make him think I was a prowler," Don said. "Well, my dad grabbed my hand, pulled it off his mouth— I couldn't believe how strong he was. So, anyway, he pulls it off his mouth and says in his regular voice tone, 'Son, don't even think about ever doing this again.'

"So, no, I didn't get him that time."

Don had to explain the story to the police, who, like his father, didn't find a lot of humor in it.

But revenge time did come, not long thereafter. His father, who also is named Don, but has a different middle name from his son, often worked long hours, or multiple jobs, to take care of his family. The five children's mother, Barb, worked at the local school.

So one night, Don's father was coming home from work

at the utility company. Don saw the headlights, and snuck down in the garage, hiding under a car his father had to walk by to get in the house.

"He never hopped out of his work truck right away," Don said. "He signed off on the radio with the dispatcher, and told the dispatcher to have a good night. So he gets out, and when he's walking by the car, I reach out from underneath and grabbed his ankle. Scared him to death. Even he'll admit that one."

"Yeah," his father said, "he got me."

The best stories about Beebe's competitive side originate on the golf course, where he can be just unbearable, according to Chadron State College head football coach Brad Smith, who stays in close touch with Don.

"We were at one of those indoor golf facilities when Don was in Buffalo with the Bills," Smith recalls. "We stood there and argued about who was closer to the pin for, well, it must have been about 15 minutes. He thought he was closer to the hole. Finally, I just gave in."

"I don't really remember that," Don said. "But if Brad said it happened, it probably did. And I can guarantee you that I was closer to the hole."

Don's agents, Bob and Lynn LaMonte, accompanied Beebe to a celebrity golf tournament for charity at Lake Tahoe in the summer of 1997, after the Packers won the Super Bowl. Bob caddied for Don. Lynn, Bob's wife, knew their client was competitive, but worked to contain it.

"He was just getting unbearable," Lynn recalls with a par five smile. "I mean, he was being a baby. Just way, way too serious and getting worked up for no real reason. I called him a putz."

"I could not believe she called me a putz," Don said. "I just looked at her, and we couldn't stop laughing."

Was Don being a putz?

"It's hard to say," Don said. "But she did call me a putz.

"Only God knows why I'm as competitive as I am. But there is one thing that I'm completely sure of, and that is that I don't have to compete for God's love, peace, and joy. It is a gift. We don't compete for it because it's a battle already fought on the cross. We can win and have victory forever."

Don's parents: Don and Barb Beebe. "Mom and Dad, truly the greatest parents God has made."

The Beebes (top): Diana, Amanda, MaKayla, Don, and Chad. Below: Amanda at age 5, Chad at age 2, and MaKayla at age 1.

The Beebe Family at Beth's wedding, 1980. Left to right: Dave, Don, Beth, Mom, Dad, Diane, and Dan.

The Beebe Family at Dave's Wedding. Left to right: Dan, Diane, Dad, Mom, Dave, Beth, and Don.

The Beautiful Women of the Beebe Family. Left to right, back row: Beth Harner (sister), Mandy Beebe (sister-in-law), Stacy Beebe (sister-in-law); front row: Diana (Don's wife) and Diane McQuade (sister).

"I couldn't ask for two better brothers." Don (left), Dave (middle), and Dan (right).

Four generations from Grandma Kuhl to Amanda. "My grandma had dreamed of watching me play in a Super Bowl. On January 26, 1992 in her home, Grandma's dream came true. Just a few short hours later she passed away to be with the Lord. Thank you, God, for a dream come true.

Two of Don's favorite ladies: Joyce Glass, owner of the resort where the Beebe's have vacationed for 28 years, and her daughter, Kay Erickson.

Beebe and childhood friend, Jeff Erickson, whose family owns Don's favorite fishing lake in Minnesota.

Don's favorite place here on earth: The lake in Minnesota
where his family has vacationed for 28 years.

Don and Diana at their favorite lake in Minnesota in 1982.
"Look at my hair!" Don and his dad with a string of bass.
"Of course, mine is the biggest!"

"My dad taught me how to filet fish at an early age so he wouldn't have to do it." Autrain, Michigan, 1976.

Don and sister Diane, 1982. "We still argue whose fish is bigger."

Don at age 10. Just another day at the lake.

A proud father with his daughter. Amanda the Bass Master catches her first big one! 3 lbs. 17 inches.

Don and Diana Beebe and Bob and Lynn LaMonte, Don's agents, celebrating the Packers' Super Bowl victory.

Don at the Lake Tahoe CGA Golf Tournament. Left to right: Mookie Blaylock, Don, Mike Eruzione, and Bob LaMonte, Don's caddy for the event.

3

BEGINNING
A CHRISTIAN WALK

Don Beebe did not become a born-again Christian when he signed his first million-dollar contract—although he insists he judges no one when it comes to when they become saved.

But the roots of Don's deep faith began to take a strong hold when he was just a little boy.

"I became a born-again Christian when I was seven years old," Don said. "I was sitting in a pew in church. The pastor said, 'If anyone wants to accept Christ you can come up to the altar and ask Jesus into your life, if you want to.'

"I knew what it meant. I was sitting with my Aunt Marian. She went up there with me. After I asked Jesus into my life, she asked me, 'Is there anything you want to ask

God right now?' I said, 'Yes, I'd like to ask God if I could be something special in sports.'

"I didn't know where that would take me. I didn't know what that would pertain to. I was just a sports nut, and I wanted to be good at it. It's ironic how things have turned out. God answered that prayer. I went through grade school and high school and enjoyed all sports."

But after his sophomore year, his interest in football was waning. He decided to forego football, working instead on honing his basketball skills in hopes of earning a college scholarship.

"I had it all figured out," Don said. "I'd work on my game, and have a great year in basketball."

His father really did have it all figured out.

"I'm a dad, and I know a college scholarship is hard to come by," his father said. "I knew he was good at basketball, but he was small. If he was going to make it in sports —and he maintained he was going to do sports in college— it was going to be football, with that speed of his."

But his father didn't make Don go out for football.

"I told him he could go out for cross country," his father said with a smile. "I said, 'Cross country is a great conditioning sport. You'll be all ready for basketball after cross country.'"

"If it wasn't for Dad forcing me," Don says with a laugh, "I wouldn't have gone out for football. He said, 'Son if you don't go out for football, you're going out for cross country.' That limited my choices, so I picked football. It was awful. I hated every minute of it. We were 1-8."

Don wasn't really looking forward to it his senior year,

either.

"My senior year rolled around, and my senior friends and buddies were looking forward to it," Don said. "I was looking more forward to basketball season."

Don credits his high school coach, Joe Thorgesen, with helping Don get his enthusiasm back.

"Coach said, 'We're going to get you the ball, you're going to be the featured running back,'" Don recalls. "We started out 6-0. It was just great."

The season ended at 6-3, but one of those wins was over Morris High School, a bitter rival never before beaten by Kaneland, Don's high school. Beebe threw a halfback pass to one of his friends, Todd Gramly, to clinch the win.

"That was the greatest win," Don says. "Don't get me wrong, the Super Bowls are great. But to never beat a team in school history, and for us to finally do it in that fashion was pretty exciting."

Football ended, and Don, still small at 165 pounds, didn't draw a lot of interest.

"I got letters from state schools," he said. "No one really showed interest except Western Illinois. They offered me a full ride, everything paid for, which is a father's dream— not necessarily my dream. Basketball was still my first love, but because of Coach (Joe) Thorgesen, I developed a love for football."

First day of school. Little Donnie Beebe stands in front the family home in Sugar Grove, Illinois, waiting to leave for his first day in school, 1970.

Groovy Don in the 8th grade. "Check out the hair, will ya?"

Don in his senior year of high school. He was the starting tailback on the Kaneland Knights.

Don's high school buddies and high school coaches at his and Diana's wedding in 1988. Back row left to right: Bruce Peterson (head track coach), Ralph Drendel (track coach), Joe Thorgesen (head football coach), Bob Pederson (head basketball coach), Rick Dalton (basketball coach), Rick Thorgesen (quarterback), and Doug Wise (center). Front row left to right: Mike Walker (tight end), Todd Gramly (split end), Don, Scott Sheridan (guard), and Greg Kramer (cornerback).

4

CAMP CRADDOCK: WESTERN ILLINOIS UNIVERSITY, 1983

Since Western Illinois was the only college to offer a full scholarship, Don's options were fairly limited. That first fall, entering camp in 1983 as a 165-pound running back, is an experience he will never forget.

Bruce Craddock, a former Marine captain in Vietnam, was the head coach at Western Illinois. It was Craddock's first season. And it is a year no one associated with the program will ever forget either. Craddock, a 6'2", 230-pounder, still had quite a bit of the Marine Corps in him when he enlisted in the college coaching ranks.

"He ran football camp like a boot camp," Don said. "It

was just awful—the worst two weeks of my life. I wasn't keen on leaving home and Diana at that time anyway. It was at least 95 degrees for two straight weeks, and for humidity, it was the worst summer of all time—at least for those two weeks."

Eager to make a good first impression, Beebe was ready to show his speed during the first drill, the 40-yard dash. But it ended up being dashes, because every drill was plural for Craddock.

"He made us run 40-yard dashes until we puked," Don said. "And I never puke. The first few, I was going to show him how fast I was. The first 10, I won. The last 8, I was bringing up the rear."

"I called Diana every night," Don said. "She cried, and I cried. I could not eat. The only thing I could do was drink water. I'd go to the cafeteria, the mess hall is what they called it. Everyone else was gorging themselves with food. I couldn't eat. If I did, it was diarrhea, and I was in the bathroom all night—it was miserable. I don't know how I made it without killing myself for a lack of nutrition. The way we were practicing, you had to have some sort of nutrition."

Todd Auer was a freshman fullback in Beebe's class.

"We used to make fun of Don, calling home all the time," said Auer, now Chadron State College's defensive coordinator.

But not too much fun, according to Bill O'Boyle, a sophomore that year at Western Illinois. "We were all calling home crying, and Todd might not admit it, but he was in that group too," said O'Boyle, also an assistant at

Chadron State. "We'd meet at night, and everyone would want to quit. That camp was a nightmare."

Craddock didn't wear a helmet, but that didn't stop him from head-butting players who were wearing helmets.

"Not just little head butts to get attention," O'Boyle said. "But banging heads hard. He would knock players down sometimes. Any other man would've split his head. Not Crad."

Auer remembers even then that Beebe's speed was unique. "I was a fullback, and I was supposed to block for Don on drills. He was past me before I'd hit the line of scrimmage. I mean, he was just too fast, it was kind of un-believable."

The camp became worse by the day for Beebe.

"The day came when I finally drew the line," he said. "We were having a bad practice, and Coach Craddock got mad at us. He said, 'All right guys, follow me. You don't want to practice—follow me. We'll take a little trip.' "

A little trip turned into a six-mile run, with pads and helmets on. When the team returned after penance for the bad practice, things didn't improve.

"We got back and were still practicing badly—ob-viously, we were dead tired," Don said. "So he's really mad now. So we sprint across the campus to a hay field. He said, 'Circle the wagons! Circle the wagons!' So we're all circled around him, a huge circle. He wants us to do this drill where we stomp our feet, hit the ground, and pop back up. He said we were going to do 20 as long as everyone did it right and kept up. We didn't get it right. The last count I remember was 114, and this is in a hay field, helmets on, 98 degrees, humidity high, mouthpieces in. Last I remember, I was salivating at the mouth. I couldn't keep my mouthpiece in my mouth. Linemen were falling on the ground.

"From that day on, I said, 'I'll never play this sport again in my life. I hate this.' Every night, I'd call Mom and Dad. The first few days, Mom was like, 'It's okay, honey, it's not that bad, you'll get used to it'. A week or two into it, I'm like, 'No, I'm serious, I'm coming home.' Mom was like, 'Maybe you should come home.' Dad said, 'Son, you're not coming home, you'll get used to it.' I said, 'Dad, I'm coming home.'"

His mother said the time had come for Don to come home. "He said that either we come get him or he'd walk home," Barb said.

His father still thought it was a mistake.

"Dad never really did give into it," Don said. "He was upset with it. It hurt our relationship for a while. He knew that I was throwing something away that only comes to a few kids in the world. But at that time I couldn't see the future like he could. I hated it. I wasn't going to keep doing what I was doing. I had lost 20 pounds in two weeks, and I wasn't that big to begin with. I was 145 pounds then. My cheeks were sunken in. When they picked me up, they didn't recognize me."

Don said he respected Craddock, but wasn't ready to join the Corps, so to speak. "He'd head butt you when you had a helmet on," Don said, repeating O'Boyle's story. "One time, we flew to Fresno State. We landed in Fresno, and the door opened up, and he was acting like he was jumping—a leatherneck jumping out of a plane going to war. He jumped out without the stairs there. He just jumped onto the concrete, landed, and hit his head. He got up and said, 'Let's go, Leathernecks!' He was just nuts."

The unique deplaning had its roots long before Beebe's one and only season at Western Illinois.

"We went up to Northern Michigan for a game, and maybe this was Crad's first time doing it, because it was by accident," Auer said. "It was one of those stair things that they drive over to the side of the jet and roll it up close. Well, we're getting ready to get off the plane, and Crad says, 'Wait, it could be an ambush—a trap! No one goes until I'm on the ground.' Well, Crad missed the first step, and goes falling flat on the ground, hits his head and everything. He gets up, starts beating his chest and yells, 'They can't hurt me! They can't hurt us!' It was funny, because he's going off, and he's got this rip in his pants. He gets all quiet and says, 'Oh, no, my wife's going to be mad at me because I ripped my pants.'"

Beebe's future coach at Chadron State, Brad Smith, was the quarterback coach at Western Illinois when Don attended WIU for the first time. After Beebe had left in the fall of his freshman year, Smith remembers Craddock's motivational speech before a home game.

"There was this wooden fan in the locker room," Smith said. "Our equipment guy had made it at home—it was an old hog farm fan. It was home-made, with no screen or anything like that. Just the blade and the wooden frame. Well, we're in the locker room before the game, and the players are lined up. Craddock wants to get the emotion up, so he starts giving his 'Never, never give up' speech that he gave before every game. Then, he grabs the fan, and picks it up, just ripping the plug out of the wall. Crad smashes the fan over his head, which broke the wood to pieces. The blade cut Crad's head up—he was bleeding. Luckily, the fan had come unplugged when he picked it up, so the blade wasn't moving very fast when he broke it over his head. The players went crazy—you could hear a roar coming from the room. But some of the players just looked at each other in disbelief—I know I was in that group, too. You always had to be on your toes when Crad gave a pre-game speech. You never knew what was going to go flying."

Don said Craddock didn't just stand there and bark out orders during practices. "He wouldn't just make us run —he'd lead the pack," Don said. "He'd outrun everybody. He'd be singing military marching songs. Someone would get hurt, and he wouldn't call for a trainer. He would yell, 'Medic! Medic!' It was quite a scene. I've never seen anything like it. I won't again."

When practice didn't have the intensity Craddock wanted, he'd stop practice.

"He'd lead us on runs, like five- or six-mile runs," Auer recalls. "Well, one time he takes us through the archery course, and at the very end is a big target. Crad goes headfirst into it—would've broken anyone else's neck right then and there. But he bounces back off of it and gets all fired up. He cut his head, and said his wife would be mad at him for that. Aside from that, he was fine. You'd take a bullet for the man, he was such a motivator."

Another time, Craddock called out to "Circle the

wagons!" and asked if anyone on the team had the guts to knock him off the top of a tackling dummy that was lying sideways on the ground.

"One of our guys came out of nowhere, and just blind-sided Crad," Auer said. "We all dog piled him, just pounded him. And Crad was yelling, 'Yes, yes, that's the kind of fight! Bring it on!' You just had to see it to believe it."

Don said while he personally has no military experience, he can't imagine that the Marines' boot camp was much tougher than Camp Craddock.

"We'd do drills for two hours that other teams did for a couple of minutes," Don said.

One was a stance-and-sprint drill, where players crouch down in their stance and then sprint out 10 yards.

"One day," Don said, "We did a thousand of them. I started getting tired. My butt was getting high. Coach Crad walked behind me and says, 'What kind of stance is that, son? Your butt's too high!' And he kicked me right in the butt, so hard I ended up sprawled out, spread eagle. I was like, 'Dang, my dad didn't even do that.' He definitely got his point across. He taught me how to work hard."

Craddock passed away only six years later, a victim of cancer. According to Auer, who saw him up to the day he died, Craddock asked about his players every time. Don said there was little else in the world that could've brought Craddock down.

"Cancer—that was the only thing that could kill that man," Don said. "Nothing else could've ever gotten him."

A Western Illinois Leatherneck wide receiver in 1987.

Coach Bruce Craddock had a great influence on Don.

5

HOOP DREAM?

Where to from Camp Craddock? How about college basketball?

Beebe walked on at Aurora College and started on the JV team as a freshman, and was the team's leading scorer.

"I liked basketball better than football, especially then," Don remembers.

But he liked little else at Aurora when he wasn't playing hoops. "I enjoyed it," Don said. "But I wasn't really into the college scene. I wasn't into partying, so I was bored. I wasn't into schoolwork. I was just into sports, not doing schoolwork. I started skipping class. I was like, 'Why am I doing this, wasting my time?'"

So toward the end of the spring semester in 1984, Beebe called his brother-in-law, Bob McQuade, who owned a siding business, and asked for a job. He got it. Don liked installing the aluminum siding, and he had money for the first time in several years.

"I thought, 'Shoot, I'll do that for a couple of years and see what happens,'" Don said. "I did it for almost three years. But I did take the time and effort to stay in shape."

But the football itch was coming back. Beebe came to the point where he couldn't watch football on television without thinking about what he could do if he was on the field.

"In the summer of 1986, I started talking to Bob every day about sports," Don said. "I said, 'I need to go back to school, I need to play football.' I felt I was fast enough. I was dreaming that I could play in the NFL."

The talk of pro sports shifted to Beebe's first love of basketball—and even to baseball—as he and Bob went through all the sports, discussing whether they were realistically a part of Don's future or not.

"Bob and I were just talking, you know, stupid guy talk," Don said. "He said, 'You could play for the Cubs. You could steal bases. And you could learn to hit.' You have to understand, Bob is a big baseball fan, and he used to be a pretty good player, too."

In May of 1986, the Chicago Bears were having their annual mini-camp at Lake Forest College in Illinois.

"Bob talked me into it," Don said. "He said, 'Why don't you try out for the Bears?' He talked me into going down there—to see if I could walk on with the Bears! Bob said, 'Go see if you can find a coach or someone there to time you in the 40 (yard dash). Maybe then, they'll sign you.'"

It sounded good, at least to a couple of guys who were passing the time while installing aluminum siding. However, the NFL isn't big on siding guys.

"I was led by the spirit of God to go back," Don said. "I don't know what it entailed, but I had a calling."

So McQuade got Beebe to go.

"Naive as I was, I said, all right and I went by myself," Don said.

He showed up at camp, and quickly realized that not only had he missed the open tryout, that there in fact was no such thing as an open tryout and he would be little more, in fact nothing more, than a spectator.

"They had stands set up, and I was sitting there alone," Don said.

Low and behold, against all odds, who shows up? The general manager of the Chicago Bears.

"I was a big Bears fan, so I knew who Bill Tobin was, the general manager," Don said. "He was sitting up behind me two rows. Now, to understand what happens next, you have to know me.

"I'm not a guy to go out of the way to talk to somebody, especially if I don't know who you are. And especially not to a guy in that position. I'm not a guy who can sell myself —I could never be my own agent. Something—and I don't know what it was—made me turn around and talk to him."

"Mr. Tobin," Don said, drawing the GM's attention. "How do you get a tryout?"

Tobin looked at Beebe, and tried to put on a nice face, maybe searching for a quick answer to make the conversation shorter. "We don't take guys off the street," Tobin said. "You have to be invited to camp."

Beebe persisted, which was unusual, especially considering how he is around complete strangers, much less someone with the clout of Tobin.

"What if I could run a 4.2 or 4.3 40-yard dash for you? Would you sign me?" Don asked.

At that point, Beebe had yet to be timed in the 40-yard dash. But he knew what a good time was, and simply figured that's about where he'd fall in line.

Tobin looked at Beebe, perhaps with equal parts disbelief and shock. "Son, if you could run a 4.2 or 4.3 40, you'd already be in our camp or someone else's camp," Tobin said.

"Oh," Don replied. "Okay."

That ended the conversation.

"I left kind of dejected that I didn't get a tryout or anything," Don said, before adding with a smile, "that also ended my career with the Chicago Bears."

But his career as a siding installer had also wound down.

"He was making a good living at it," said Diana. "But he wasn't fulfilled. The Lord spoke to his heart."

Beebe made another momentous decision in his life. He decided to return to Western Illinois.

Don's senior year at Kaneland High School, 1983.
"Basketball is my favorite sport."

6

RETURN TO
CAMP CRADDOCK
AND WESTERN ILLINOIS

Again low on options for salvaging his football career, Beebe was at peace with returning in the fall of 1987 to Western Illinois and Coach Craddock.

"The other coaches and players said Crad had lightened up," Don said. "The coaches had called out of the blue, after I had thought about going back while I was hanging siding. I knew the Lord wanted me to. The coaches said they wanted me to come back. That was an answer to a prayer. But I was still apprehensive because I had such a bad experience before."

"I remember when I first left, Brad Smith, the quarterback coach, and Mike Williams, the running backs coach, begged me not to leave. I was crying, and they were pretty emotional, too. But when I went back, I felt good about it."

But since he had started college in 1983, his NCAA eligibility time, five academic school years to play four seasons of football, a time frame which started the first day a student enrolled, had run on, and almost, as it was learned, run out.

"A coach told me on the phone that I needed to know that my eligibility clock kept running," Don said. "Once I came to school and started classes, my eligibility had started. It turned out I had two years left. I called and said I'm coming back (in the fall of 1986)."

In a decision that turned out to be in error, Beebe was declared ineligible by the school's NCAA representative, who misinterpreted a rule regarding transfers.

"Toward the end of football camp, the NCAA faculty representative (James McKinney) called me into his office and said, 'Don, we're going to declare you ineligible for this year.' I asked why. He told me I was 4.5 credit hours short of being a transfer," Don recalls. "I was like, 'That can't be.' I felt like God wanted me back here. They said they wanted me to get the credits and come back."

Rather than drop football once and for all, Beebe pushed forward, knowing it was late in the game as far the NCAA was concerned and feeling he had few choices left when it came to schools.

"I still had some hope," he said. "But, basically I was a kid without a school. I went to Waubonsee (Ill.) Junior College for a semester. I transferred back in the spring of

1987 to start classes."

Coming back for the spring ended up being the first step to the NFL. But like just about everything else in Beebe's life, the route was neither well-marked nor likely. Each afternoon after his final class, Don walked from a class room building, around—never through—the gymnasium, to his dorm.

"Everyday, I came out of my class, and I never, not even one time, had walked through the Western Illinois Activities Center. I never walked through the building," Don said. "That day, I just decided to walk through the building. I was in jeans shorts, a tank top, and sandals. Some of my teammates, who were seniors, were being timed in the 40-yard dash by NFL scouts. I hadn't played, so I didn't know anything about it. But, as it turned out, they were all seniors, and the scouts had game film on them. I was a senior, but I hadn't played college football, so there was no film."

Beebe walked up to Coach Craddock. "Coach, I want to run for the scouts," Don said.

Craddock resisted.

"He told me basically not to waste my time," Don said.

The coach said he didn't think Beebe could because this had been set up in advance. But Beebe persisted, and the coach went to ask a scout.

"Yeah, Don, you can run," coach said. "You can go ahead and run."

Beebe looked down at his feet and his jeans shorts, and then saw his teammates in running shoes and running shorts.

"Coach, we have one more problem," Don said to Craddock. "I don't have my track shoes or running shoes to run on the track. I don't have time to go back to my dorm room."

"Look, Donny," Craddock said. "I don't want to ask them if you can go get your shoes. They'll be done timing in just a minute anyway."

"So I didn't have time to get my shoes," Don recalled. "He said, 'Look Donny, just run it without your sandals.'"

Beebe, barefoot, ran just over 4.3 seconds, a record for the track at that time.

"I ran the fastest time ever on that track, a 4.3," Don said. "If you could've heard me running down the track—pitter-pattering—barefoot."

After the players ran, they would put sweats on over their shorts, change from their running shoes to street shoes or kick-around sneakers, and head for the door.

"Everybody would run , come back put their clothes on and leave," Don said. "No one ever got talked to. After I ran, the Dallas Cowboys scout called me over."

"Son, what's your name?" the scout asked.

"I'm Don Beebe."

"What number are you on the game film?" the scout asked.

"I'm a fifth-year senior," Don said. "But I never played football here, or anywhere else, before. I sat out and worked."

The scout looked around in astonishment. "What?" he asked. "Well, you ran a great time. We'll keep an eye on you."

"That," Don said, "is where it all started with the NFL."

Buoyed by his contact with the scout, Beebe, who moved to wide receiver, was a standout during the spring practice session.

"We're a month or two into school, doing spring drills, and I ended up doing pretty well in camp," Don said. "The NCAA representative from our school calls me back into his office at the end of spring drills."

Beebe felt knocked off his feet when McKinney spoke. "The coaches and I have decided not to give you your eligibility," McKinney said.

Ready to leave school, Don started to cry.

"The dreams and aspirations I had were now done," Don said. "What this guy told me brought me to the end of my journey. Looking back, they might've thought, 'What's this going to look like to the NCAA? This kid comes in, he's never played before, and he's catching passes and doing well.'"

McKinney tried to console Beebe.

"I know you want to play," he told Don. "But it's not solely my decision."

"The guy just felt terrible," Don said.

Needing Diana and his family, Don went back to his dorm room. During the following five hours, he got completely packed, loaded up his car, and cleaned his dorm room, which was required of students before they could check out.

"I was getting kicked out of school," Don said.

As Beebe picked up a final load to take to his car, the phone rang before he turned out the light. With a hand on the door, he listened to it ring, and decided there was no point in answering it.

"I wasn't even going to pick it up," Don said. "I was upset, and I was pretty sure it was a family member or friend who was going to tell me I'd be all right. But I had talked to a bunch of people at that point, and I didn't feel like talking any more, to anyone, on the phone."

Oddly, the phone didn't stop ringing.

"I felt like the Holy Spirit was saying, 'Pick up the phone,'" Don said. "It was McKinney on the phone."

"Come back to my office," he told Don. "I might have some good news."

Beebe set down his bag.

"Obviously, I was excited," Don said. "I went right over."

McKinney had a stack of papers. Sitting on top of the papers was the NCAA eligibility manual, which is much more like a big book than a manual.

"Don, I've been sitting here for five hours, trying to find the eligibility rules," McKinney said.

McKinney picked up the book and showed Beebe the rule, which was in small-size type on a big page full of rules. It stated that once a student-athlete enrolled in a school, if they come back—to the same school—they are not considered a "transfer" student, simply a re-entry student, regardless of whether they attended any other schools in the interim.

"So, as it turned out," Don recalls, "I could've played in 1986. At that point, it didn't matter. Obviously, it was the Lord working it out so I could play one year."

The way it all turned out was the work of the Lord.

"This is the part that's mind boggling to me," Don said. "The Lord worked it out. Why did McKinney spend five hours trying to find eligibility for a kid who had never even played college ball, is only going to be at the school one year, and play a position, wide receiver, where it takes two years to learn the position? Obviously, the Lord felt to complete my journey, I had to close the circle at Western Illinois."

Don's homesickness for Diana was eased by his younger brother, Dan, who during his freshman year roomed with him in the dorm during Don's final year at Western Illinois.

"We were away from home, and it was just me and him," Dan said. "We really grew close that year."

Still, Don's competitive side was always visible, even away from the football field.

"There was a hardcourt to play basketball on just outside of our dorm, Wetzel Hall," Dan said. "We'd just school everybody. We'd play one on one, but we actually got away from that because it was too competitive. We couldn't play against each other anymore, it just wasn't fun. If we played 5-on-5, we couldn't guard each other, it was just too much."

With no more surprises hiding within either the confines of the NCAA rule book or at Camp Craddock, Beebe enjoyed a standout fall at Western Illinois, earning All-Conference honors.

"I had a pretty good season," Don said. "It wasn't great or anything, but it caught some people's attention. Some scouts came back in. They said they liked the way I ran and caught the ball. But they said with only one year of college football to my name, they couldn't use a draft pick on me, that I'd have to be signed as a free agent. Now, I was fine with that. I said, 'That's all I need with God on my side, a free-agent shot.'"

An assistant coach pointed out that the NAIA would allow Beebe at least another year.

"There's another avenue you could take," said Assistant Coach Randy Ball. "All the scouts are complaining that you only have one year, that you don't have enough experience. You could go to the NAIA, which is totally separate from the NCAA."

At that point, however, Beebe did not know what the NAIA acronym stood for (National Association of Inter-collegiate Athletics), much less know of any NAIA schools. He did learn that, unlike the NCAA, which starts the clock the first-day a student athlete enrolls and gives him five years to complete four years of eligibility, the NAIA goes by 10 semesters. Those 10 do not run straight through, meaning an athlete could leave school indefinitely, and return, with eligibility intact. However, to be eligible, the athlete must successfully complete a full-time student course load for one semester before becoming eligible.

"But even after more than four years, I only had been in school for four semesters," Don said. "So I had at least two years left in the NAIA."

That sounded workable to Beebe.

"With God on my side," Don said. "I felt I could accomplish anything."

7
WHERE TO NEXT?

Beebe entered Christmas break on a high note. Still, there was apprehension because he had to find an NAIA school.

"Christmas is only a three-week break," Don said. "I talked it over with Mom, Dad, and Diana. We figured that's what the Lord wanted me to do. I was a little older, but it seemed like that was the thing to do because at this point it was only a free agent shot."

So, there was a lot of work to be done in a short period of time.

"Dad, do you know of any NAIA schools?"

"No, Don," his father responded. "Do you?"

Beebe and his father went to the library and looked up the NAIA colleges in the region. However, the school had to meet four requirements:

1. It needed to be close to home.

2. The school had to have posted a good record last season.

3. The school had to be in a position to get national exposure so scouts will see him play.

4. The school must be pass oriented with an experienced, talented quarterback.

"We found one in Michigan, but we still had a lot of looking to do," Don said. "And then Illinois Benedictine called, and it was about perfect. It was so close I could have commuted—about 10 minutes. They had a good record. They had a quarterback who was back after throwing for more than 3,000 yards as a junior the previous year."

That night, the phone rang. Brad Smith, the former quarterback coach at Western Illinois, who had left before what turned out to be Beebe's one and only season at WIU, was on the line.

"Donny," Smith said. "Coach Ball called me and said you're looking for an NAIA school."

"Yeah, I am," Don replied. "Do you know of one?"

"I'm the coach of one," Smith said.

"Great," Don said. "Where are you coaching at?"

Beebe was excited about playing for one of his former coaches, one who had tried to talk him into staying at Western Illinois during the first Camp Craddock. Smith was very compassionate and seemed to have Don's interest at heart back then, so Beebe thought this might be a good option.

"I'm at Chadron State College," Smith said.

"Shhhh-what?" Don said.

Chadron is pronounced "Shad-run".

"Chadron, Don. Chadron State. It's in Nebraska," Smith said.

Beebe didn't know Chadron from Chevron, although he could properly pronounce Chevron.

"Get out your atlas," Smith said.

Beebe did, turning to the Nebraska page. He looked at the page and saw Omaha…Grand Island…Lincoln…but no Chadron.

"Coach, I see Omaha and Lincoln, but no Chadron," Don said.

"Don, look way up in the northwest corner," Smith instructed.

Beebe did. Only one dot was in the northwestern most corner of the state. And there wasn't anything else around it. So, basically, Don thought if you could get to the middle of nowhere, and didn't mind the trip, Chadron wouldn't be hard to find.

Beebe started shaking his head toward his father. Better to end the conversation now before he gets even one step closer to no-man's land.

"Well, coach," Don said, "thanks for calling."

"No, Don, don't hang up, wait a minute," Smith said. "You are an outdoorsman. You'll love it here."

Beebe said Smith went on to sell Chadron like a flood insurance salesman in the desert. There simply wasn't anything to discuss.

"Coach, I'll give you this—I'll pray on it," Don said. "But I seriously doubt I'm going to come all the way out there."

Don and his father got a laugh, but little else, from the call. Don and Diana had just gotten engaged, and the last thing on his mind was moving 14-15 hours from home. The last thing Don and Smith talked about was Don's scheduled visit to Illinois Benedictine.

"Whatever they offer you, don't let them tell you they can do all this stuff—it's an NAIA college, just like Chadron State," Smith said.

"Well, okay, coach, but I'm sorry , there's no way I'm coming out," Don said. "But like I said, I will pray on it."

Chadron State, nestled comfortably between Mount Rushmore in South Dakota, less than two hours to the north, and Scottsbluff, Nebraska roughly 100 miles to the south, still wasn't much more than a passing thought to Beebe.

"You could've paid me a million dollars," Don said, "and I wasn't going to go out there. So I hung up the phone. I remember praying that night, I was just saying, 'Please, Lord, don't send me to Chadron. I don't want to go out there.'"

Two days later, Don and his father went to Illinois Benedictine.

"The coaches were nice," Don recalls. "It was intriguing because they had everything I wanted, even a good receiver who would have started with me so I wouldn't have been double covered or anything."

At the time, Illinois Benedictine sounded almost too good to be true.

"We'll throw the ball to you a lot," an assistant coach said. "Our quarterback is really good. We're a passing team, first and only."

Beebe couldn't shake the feeling that something wasn't right.

"The coach was a nice guy," Don said. "But I never felt comfortable from the time I walked in. Yet, it was everything that we had drawn up, and even more in some ways. Just ideal."

Don and his father had lunch afterward.

"Before he opened his mouth, I knew he wasn't going," his father said. "It just wasn't right. The Lord didn't want him there."

Don confirmed his Dad's feelings. "Dad, as good as it sounds, this isn't where the Lord wants me."

That spiritual guidance didn't really make a lot of sense to Beebe at that time. But knowing it was part of a bigger plan, he gladly followed the Lord.

"No matter how good things look in the world's eyes and your eyes, it won't work out if it's not God's will," Don said. "If you're not listening to the Lord—and the only way you can listen to Him is through prayer and reading His word—you'll eventually fail. I firmly believe if I'd gone to Illinois Benedictine, I wouldn't be here in Green Bay today. I wouldn't have reached God's will for my life."

Ruling out Illinois Benedictine solved only one problem, while creating another. If not Illinois Benedictine, then where? The Lord was on Don's side, but time clearly wasn't. Don had three days to make his decision, because the spring semester was about to start and he had to be enrolled to be eligible for the fall.

"Lord, I don't know if You've had a rush job, or if You

even do rush jobs, but we have one now," Don said as he prayed.

Smith, a native of Sycamore, Illinois, headed home from Chadron the next day and was near the Beebes' home, so he visited. Smith had met the family during his time at Western Illinois. The complete salesman, Smith brought pictures of fish.

"They were fish we had caught at Ishom Lake (near Chadron)," Smith recalls. "They weren't like out of a book or anything. We have great fishing up there, and Donny likes to fish."

"I reassured Coach Smith that I wasn't coming there as he left the house," Don said. "He really did a good job, though. He laid out maps, pictures of the fish, the whole works. I was praying fervently not to go to Chadron. Yet I kept feeling that Chadron was being laid on my heart. I was like, kind of resisting it, like, 'No, Lord, please.'"

He looked at his gridiron litmus test:

1. Close to home? No, nearly 15 hours away.

2. Winning record? No, Chadron State was 1-8 the last year, Smith's first as head coach.

3. Exposure? The only exposure out there was from the elements.

4. A passing offense? Smith said yes, but the quarterback had graduated and an incoming freshman, projected as the starter, stood only 5-foot-10.

"I really thought," Smith recalls, "that I wasn't going to get this young man."

But the issue was settled.

"I finally came to the sense that Chadron is where the

Lord wanted me," Don said. "I tell people this, too, that if you follow the Lord's will, you can be in the remotest area in the world and still make it in the NFL for nine years, with five Super Bowls. I mean, really, I'm living testimony to that."

Beebe called Smith.

"I said I was coming," Don said. "Coach Smith was happy, just out of his mind."

Smith said the call would change a lot of lives, in addition to boosting Chadron State College's notoriety.

"Don said, 'Coach, how do I get to Chadron?'" Smith recalls. "If he said I was 'pretty excited,' then he was understating it."

8

FINDING MRS. RIGHT

At Western Illinois in the fall of 1983, Beebe spent hours a day thinking about his girlfriend, Diana. Same thing the first semester at Chadron in the spring of 1988, where the pain was almost bearable because they were planning to marry that summer.

Their relationship started with a kiss—in the second grade.

"They had this quiet corner in the back of the room," Diana recalls. "I just thought Donny was so cute. We were going back to the quiet corner, and I just kissed him."

Despite the early roots, the relationship didn't take hold until high school. Mainly, it was because Beebe had little interest in anything but sports. He was a standout in football, basketball, and track.

The former Diana Beckley, at the time getting ready for

her junior year at Kaneland High School, liked one of the boys on the football team—the boy she had kissed in second grade.

In August of 1981, Diana was working the dunk tank in a fund-raiser for the cheerleading squad. She confided in a friend that she wanted to go out with Don Beebe.

"It was one of those things, where before I told her, I said, 'This has to be kept a secret, the biggest secret ever,'" Diana said. "I didn't want him to find out, and I didn't want anyone else to know either."

That friend went straight to a friend of Beebe's, Greg Kramer, who insisted Beebe go see Diana at the booth.

Don related it this way. "One of Diana's best friends comes over to me and says, 'Don, you know who likes you?' I said, 'Who?' She said, 'Diana Beckley. You should ask her out. Just ask her out.' I was like, I'm not going to ask her, she'd never like me.

"I wasn't going to do it. Greg was all over me. If it wasn't for Greg Kramer, we probably wouldn't be together. Greg said, 'Dude, she's beautiful, you have to ask her out.' I said, 'Greg, I'm not going to asked her out. I'll embarrass myself. I'm too shy.' Greg was persistent. He finally just said, 'If you don't go over there, I'm going to kick your butt right now!' Everyone liked Diana. So I said, 'Fine, I'll go over there.' At that time, I had aspirations of dating her. But I was a nerd. I was such a nerd. Actually, I was just a gentleman, but it seems gentlemen are considered nerds, so that's what I was."

"I remember I didn't really think about girls much, because it was always go-go-go with sports," Don said.

"But if there's one girl I wanted to out with, it was Diana Beckley. But before the carnival, I could never have asked her out. For one thing, I hadn't asked a girl out, and I wouldn't be good at it. Secondly, she was really pretty, and way too good for me."

As destiny—and a loose-lipped friend—would have it, Beebe showed up at the dunk tank.

"I asked her if she wanted to go with a group of us later on to a pizza joint," Don said. "She said she wanted to, but she had to find someone to watch the booth for her. She was just being responsible."

Well, as it turned out, none of her friends could, or would, cover for her.

"It was my responsibility to stay at the booth," Diana said. "I wanted to go really bad. But I just couldn't."

"She was just being the responsible person that she is," Don said. Knowing how shy Beebe was, Diana said she'd like to go out some other time. But Beebe wasn't sure he would ask her out again. He wanted to, but he wasn't the kind who was much good on those kinds of things. It took all he had to even ask her out the first time.

Low and behold, the two were thrown together just a couple of days later through a freak incident.

Beebe and three of his friends were on their way to football practice, which had just started that week at Kaneland High School. A friend was driving when all of the sudden the car broke down—just a couple of houses down from where Diana Beckley lived.

"Someone said, 'Diana Beckley lives there. We could get a ride from her or someone in her family,'" Don said. "All the guys knew about the other night, and they were teasing me."

The boys went to the house of the one player who lived in that subdivision, but he wasn't home, having already left for practice. So the boys went to Diana's to see if she could run them into town to practice at the high school.

"As it turned out, I was just heading to the school to turn in the money from the dunk tank at the carnival," Diana said.

"She had this baby light blue Duster, and when we all went out to get in the car, the guys got in the back and I sat up front with her," Don said. "They all really thought she was cool and wanted me to ask her out."

"Actually, what happened was the guys jumped in the back of the car, and Don didn't have a choice but to sit up front," Diana said.

They got to the high school, and the boys in the back of the car scooted out the door, pushing to leave Don behind with Diana.

"I kind of hung back with her," Don said.

They walked in the school talking.

"I remembered that the night at the carnival, she did say she wanted to go out, but that she just couldn't that one night," Don said. "So I asked her again if she'd like to get some pizza and a movie."

Don pulled out all the stops, even borrowing his parents' white station wagon (did someone say nerd?). Then, her parents fell for Don as hard as Diana had.

"I said, 'Mr. Beckley, when would you like your daughter home tonight,'" Don said. "Mrs. Beckley just fell

over, just loving it. Her Dad said by 11 p.m. I said that I'd
have her home by that time.

"So we get in the car and I'm driving," Don said. "She's
sitting by the door. It's a bench seat, and she's pretty far
away."

"Don puts his arm across the seat behind me and said,
'You can sit closer, or do I stink?'" Diana remembers. For
the record, Diana did, in fact, sit close. And Beebe did not,
in fact, stink. The conversation, company, and food were
good.

"The conversation was unbelievable," Don said. "Love
right away. I knew this was the girl I wanted to spend the
rest of my life with."

Before long, Don "Not Juan" Beebe made his move.

"Now comes the moment of the good-night kiss," Don
said. "I open the door to let her into the house. I shook her
hand and said, 'Thanks for a good evening.'"

What happened next remains a point of contention.

"She leaned over and kissed me," Don said.

"He kissed me," Diana insisted. "Or at least it was
mutual."

"Actually, I think you said, 'You can kiss me if you want
to,'" Don claimed. "So I kissed her, actually on the cheek."

"It was awkward for him, I could tell," Diana said.

They almost ended up together the year before. Both
were nominated for Sophomore Homecoming Royalty.
Don asked someone to go, just as friends, while Diana also
had a date. Of course, in a story with more twists than a
bag of pretzels, they both won, sophomore king for Don,
and his queen was Diana.

"We had to dance together because we won," Diana said. "It was the best dance of the whole night."

"I remember going home that night, and my mom asked about the evening," Don said. "I said, 'The best thing about it was Diana Beckley.'"

That wasn't all he said. Don's sisters, Beth and Diane, and his mother, Barb, remember his words verbatim.

"Don said, 'Mom! Mom! You should've seen Diana Beckley. SHE'S SO HOT!'" the sisters chimed in unison.

"He was yelling," Beth said.

"Everyone could hear him," Diane said. "He said, 'She's so hot,' several times."

"Maybe I did say that," Don said sheepishly. "But you have to understand, she really was hot. So yeah, I guess I did say that."

Before he made the decision to return to Western Illinois, Beebe had some business to resolve in his personal life. He and Diana had drifted apart during the past six months as he focused his energies on everything except his relationship with Diana.

"His first love was sports," Diana said. "I was glad he loved sports, and I wanted him to continue to love sports. But if he didn't love me more than he loved sports, then I didn't want to date him any more. I loved him so much more than that."

"I wanted to hang out with the guys, play basketball—I put her on the shelf," Don remembers. "It wasn't partying or anything like that—it was just sports. She didn't understand that, and rightfully so. She got tired of that. She said, 'Either I'm going to come first or nothing.' She broke up with me and started dating another guy, a guy I knew. When she did that, she opened up my eyes bigtime. I was devastated."

"I knew in my heart how much I loved him," Diana said, "and how desperately I wanted it to work."

Diana's heart belonged to Don, so she stopped seeing the other guy she had dated for a month in the spring of 1987. She and Don got back together then. As their relationship progressed, Beebe set up a special date with her for August 8, 1987, just before he was to leave for football camp at Western Illinois. In the days leading up to the date, he was as elusive as he ever was on the football field.

"I had this planned out," Don said. "We had dated for six years. If she knew we were going to downtown Chicago, she would know I was going to propose. I made it look like I was going to take her out to break up. It wasn't something cruel, I wanted to be spontaneous, unpredictable."

"I thought he was going to break up with me," Diana said. "He wouldn't return my calls. I even went to his mother and told her I could sense he was going to break up."

His mother knew full well that her son wasn't going to break up with Diana. Quite the contrary, he was going to propose marriage.

"But I couldn't let on to the fact that I knew," Barb said. "And I did want to tell her. It pained me to see her suffering. But Don made me promise."

So they went to downtown Chicago.

"I took her to the most expensive place in Chicago," Don said. "And at that time in my life, I had almost no money. So it was a big deal."

Beebe had it all planned out. During the ride in a horse-drawn-buggy, he would propose to Diana.

"Didn't happen," Don said. "The driver never stopped talking the whole ride. I couldn't believe it. He didn't close his mouth for a second. It ruined that opportunity."

They went back to Don's car to go home. He proposed.

"I asked her in the Cutlass Supreme," Don said. "She broke down. I said, 'I hope I didn't do too much to hurt you in the last few weeks. I just wanted to set the whole thing up perfectly.'"

"We were both crying," Diana said. "It was very special."

Don's favorite car: 1985 Pontiac Cutlass Supreme.

Don's high school sweetheart, Diana Beckley, who became Mrs. Don Beebe. Diana was a cheerleader for their alma mater, Kaneland High School Knights.

Don and Diana at their senior prom at Kaneland High School. Don admits that she already had him wrapped around her little finger by this time.

9

MAKING THE RIGHT MOVE?

The family loaded into the van to take Beebe to school for the spring of 1988.

The drive through Nebraska was unspectacular to Beebe for the most part, hauling along Interstate 80 with its flat, monotonous scenery. However, exiting at Ogallala, at the start of the Nebraska Panhandle, Beebe started to enjoy the ride.

Just out of Chadron on U.S. 385, Beebe liked what he saw.

"We're driving through the national forest and Chadron State Park, and I'm like, 'This is really pretty,'" Don said. "We went through the state park and then all I saw was a Best Western and the South 40 (a restaurant-lounge) and a sign that said, Chadron: Population: 5,000. But from that ridge, you can't see the town, and I started to panic."

Don yelled from the back of the van. "Dad, where are the 5,000 people—I don't see anyone!"

His dad didn't answer.

"I heard him," his father said. "But I couldn't believe how pretty the area was."

Don, tired of being ignored and not ready to be abandoned, made a familiar pitch. "Dad, turn the van around, I'm not going here," he announced. "Let's just go right back home, right now."

His father was neither amused nor in the mood to be accommodating. The full ride awaiting him at Chadron State was Don's last shot at playing college ball, and it was a golden opportunity to finish college.

"Son, I drove you all the way out here," his dad said. "Get used to it. You are staying."

The family took a right on Main Street, and low and behold, there was human life. Not a lot, mind you, but some was better than none.

"Downtown was really nice, and there were trees," Don recalled. "The campus was pretty."

After spending all of two hours in his first dorm, Edna Works, one for non-traditional age students. "It was worse than a prison—like a jail cell or a morgue," Don said. "Concrete walls and everything." Beebe ended up in Kent Hall, and made friends.

"The first couple of weeks were tough," Don said. "Of course, I was away from Diana, and I was calling her all the time. But I was working out with the football team, started studying and I never missed class—I was a good student. I started to get a feel for Chadron—I was really starting to like the place. Where else can you drive around town and everyone waves at you? It's like, 'Hi, you are waving and you don't know me.' I was like, 'This place is great.' The people were unbelievable, the nicest I ever met."

"I still have a hard time with it," said Dan Beebe, who is now Chadron State's men's basketball coach. "People make eye contact with you here, and ask how you're doing. Where we're from, and in Chicago, people will avoid you, look down if they see you looking at them. They're just friendly here, and they really care about their neighbors."

Don wasn't real sociable, but wasn't a hermit, either.

"I'm not a partier," he said. "But I'm not a loner—I guess there's a fine line. If I get to know you, I like to hang around and have a lot of fun. But I'm not the kind of guy who goes out to meet people. I like family and close friends. Anything outside of that, I'm not real keen on."

Don went home for the summer and married Diana. While he was excited about returning to Chadron State, the couple had little money. Little brother Dan made the return trip to Chadron. Ironically, Dan had followed his brother's footsteps almost identically. After enrolling at Western Illinois and leaving, Dan installed siding, just as Don did, for a few years. Then, in a final attempt to resurrect his basketball career, Dan went with newlyweds Don and Diana to Chadron State, where he would eventually end up earning a scholarship. So Don, Diana, and Dan loaded up a U-haul trailer, attached it to Don's black Cutlass Supreme, and drove the 15 hours to the only dot on the map in northwest Nebraska.

"I had a hundred bucks in my pocket, actually we had

a hundred bucks between us, to our name," Don said. "We went out there with no place to live. I didn't have a job. Obviously, I was going to be a full-time student. Diana didn't have a job. So we had no income, no place to live, and a hundred bucks. But we had complete faith. I remember telling Diana, 'We'll be fine.' She was cool, like, yeah, we'll be all right. We went out there with complete faith that God will take care of us."

The trip ended up being a couple of hours longer than Don had remembered from the previous spring.

"We went out there, pulled into town around 10 p.m.," Don said. "We couldn't find a hotel. There were only a few, and they were closed. Diana was like, 'Where are we going to stay?' So we pulled into the football parking lot and stayed in the car that night. Thank goodness because we couldn't afford a hotel anyway."

Another sort of angel descended early the next morning as the three slept. Dan had actually gotten out of the cramped car and slept under a tree until he became too cold and had to get back in the car.

"I was walking along, and I saw this car packed full of stuff with people inside," said Marlene Myers, who was out for her morning walk. Don remembers the surprise of seeing Marlene's face in the window. Being from near Chicago, sleeping in cars was not only frowned upon, but dangerous as well.

"All of the sudden, at 6 a.m. the next morning—really at the crack of dawn, we hear a knock on the window," Don said.

"Had there been any room, I would've jumped out of

fear," Dan said.

But there wasn't any room, so Don rolled his window down.

"Are you kids lost?" Myers asked.

Don said that they were not lost, that he and his little brother were students.

"Well, do you need anything? Are you okay? Are you hungry? Do you have a place to stay?" Marlene asked.

"We don't have a place to live, and my wife needs a job," Don said.

Diana had been working for an insurance agency back in Illinois. She put in for a transfer when she found out they were moving to Chadron. But that fell through before they left Illinois.

"Well, I certainly could help you find a house," Marlene said. "And my husband (Dick) and I own Myers Drugstore downtown. We're looking for some help."

Looking back, Beebe can't believe how quickly things came together. "These are the first people we met, Dick and Marlene Myers," he said. "And they are the nicest people you ever want to meet in the world."

They went around town and looked at a couple of houses. They went to the drugstore and met Dick, who, along with Marlene, offered Diana a job. A couple of hours later, they started moving into their new house.

"It was one of those homes out back, behind another home—they call them 'Mother-in-law' houses out there," Don said. "It was just a one-bedroom house. Man, was that place great."

The house, less than a mile from the lush Nebraska

prairie, is a sort of a local historical marker now, with Beebe's fame. At that time, to Diana and Don, it was a godsend.

"A big living room and big bedroom," Don recalled. "A small kitchen and small bathroom—you could go potty and brush your teeth at the same time because your feet were underneath the sink while you were sitting there."

And the price?

"A hundred bucks a month," Don said. "We were choosing between houses that were $100, $110, $120 a month. That's just what the rent was out there. Where I'm from, you couldn't rent a doghouse for $100 a month."

"We're in town for a couple of hours, and we have a house and Diana has a job," Don said. "Incredible. Just incredible. God completely answered our prayers."

The house still holds a place in the Beebes' hearts—and they still keep a picture of it.

"It was perfect," Diana said of the house. "It was all we needed."

"From that first day, when they got moved into their house," Chadron State coach Brad Smith said, "Don said that they made the right decision to come to Chadron."

The times were lean.

"I remember paychecks for $60," Diana said. "We didn't have a lot of money. We ate a lot of macaroni and cheese, tuna, and peanut butter and jelly. And you know, it was one of the best times of our life."

When a family member sent $100, the Beebe's were able to take care of a late phone bill.

"We spent $50 dollars for the phone bill," Diana said.

"Then, with the other $50, we went and got steak. We were so excited, 'Yeah! We're getting steak!' I am so glad for those times."

Don said they had each other, and with their faith and friends in the northwestern-most outpost in Nebraska, they didn't need much more.

"Really," Don said. "We absolutely loved that place."

"The best day of my life when I married my best friend."
July, 1988.

10

Oasis in the Nebraska Panhandle

One season at Chadron State College proved to be more than enough—although Beebe could have returned for one additional year because he was still within NAIA eligibility guidelines.

The freshman quarterback, Steward Perez, ended up having plenty of arm—although the three-step drop was instituted by Smith because no one could get the ball to Beebe with anything more than the three-step.

"We didn't have anyone who could five-step drop, much less seven-step drop, and get the ball to Don," said Chris Stein, a tight end who was a teammate at Chadron State and now coaches high school football in Gering, Nebraska. "You wouldn't believe how fast he was unless you saw it in real life."

Still, Perez never heard the end of it when it came to underthrowing Beebe.

"We all used to try—everyone on the team at some point tried to outthrow him," Stein said. "But it couldn't be done. You couldn't go more than three or five steps to drop back, or the ball wouldn't get there."

Beebe was even harder on opponents. In his first game at Chadron State, against South Dakota Tech, the Eagles were struggling.

"(Quarterback) Steward Perez was struggling and had thrown five interceptions in the first half," Chadron State coach Brad Smith said. "Don came up to me at halftime and said, 'Just get the ball to me.'"

They did, and Chadron State won as Beebe caught five passes for 57 yards and ran twice for 20 yards, in addition to returning two kicks for 90 yards— 177 total yards.

"We were playing Black Hills State the next week, and their coach said he wasn't impressed," Smith said. "He said they weren't going to change anything they were doing. Their coach said, 'I don't think Beebe's all he's cracked up to be. We'll play our regular defense.'"

"The quote in the paper the week before the Black Hills game was that they didn't believe Don could run a 4.2 (40-yard dash)," Stein said. "They said they had a kid as fast as him, so they weren't going to do anything to stop him. Donny had five touchdowns that day—and there was nothing they could do to stop him."

Indeed, Beebe had seven catches for 155 yards and returned a kickoff 87 yards for a touchdown against Black

Hills State. He finished the year with 906 yards on 49 catches, and returned 27 kickoffs for 676 yards."

"We played Colorado School of Mines, and Don returned a kick that ended up being called back," Smith recalls. "But afterward, Mines' coach, Marv Kay, was in awe of Beebs. He said he didn't even see Don run by on one of the kickoffs—that Don was so fast, he was just a blur."

Chadron State information director Con Marshall writes stories and takes photos at each game, but his action file of Beebe pictures is short.

"I didn't get a lot of pictures of Don because he was so fast, and he was always so far down the field when he caught the ball," Marshall said when asked about acquiring some photos. "But we had another good receiver that year, also from Western Illinois, Mike Lockwood. He was a possession-type receiver. I have lots of pictures of him."

Beebe and his wife treasured the year in Chadron, and knew the NFL was a likelihood.

"It wasn't like the other players were that bad or anything," Diana Beebe said. "It's just that Don was so much faster."

The letters started coming into Smith's office after the season, and Beebe got some phone calls from scouts.

"After the season it was still free agent talk, maybe a late rounder, because the draft was 12 rounds then," Beebe said. "But it was all phone calls. Because no team was going to come out to Chadron."

That would change in a second—or make that 4.2 seconds, the time for Beebe in the 40-yard dash.

11

SPEED ON THE PRAIRIE

Bill Giles. That name means a lot to Don Beebe, because Giles, an NFL Combine scout (meaning he scouts for all teams) ended up being Beebe's link to NFL teams.

"I timed Don and heard from the scout who timed Don at Western Illinois," said Giles, a former coach at Chadron State. "But no one wanted to come to Chadron. So I went out and graded Don, and he ripped off at 4.3 seconds in the 40 (yard dash). Well, that looked like it had a shot at getting him into the NFL Combine."

Beebe said he actually ran faster than the 4.38.

"I went 4.28, but Bill said he couldn't put that down, because his name was on the report and if I didn't do that for other teams, it was his name and credibility," Beebe said. "But he means so much to me because he got my foot in the door. After he timed me, he said he didn't know if he could for sure, but he was going to do all he could to get me into the Combine."

The NFL Combine brings the top 300 seniors to Indianapolis for workouts and interviews with NFL coaches and general managers. Players are timed in runs and strength is measured.

It was the spring of 1989, and Beebe was getting excited. "I was anxious about whether I'd get to go, but I knew the Lord would handle it," Beebe said. "Then, I got the letter in mail."

> *Dear Don Beebe,*
>   *The NFL Combine takes this privilege to invite you to Indianapolis.*

"I was just like, oh my gosh," Beebe said. "I couldn't believe it."

Ironically, Beebe actually announced that he would not attend the Combine the night before he was supposed to leave for Indianapolis. It is referred to as the "disagreement in Chadron," just because Don and his wife Diana rarely disagree on anything, much less argue. But at that time, the newlyweds didn't see eye to eye on something—no one involved can remember the cause of the disagreement now. However, it was enough to send Don out of the house.

"You have to understand the significance of this because he and Diana never fought, they just never did," said Don's younger brother, Dan, who was a Chadron State student at the time. "They have their first fight the night before he's supposed to leave for the combine. It's 20 degrees below with the wind chill outside. He shows up without a coat, just shivering and red in the face. His hand is all swollen because he hit the wall as he walked out the door.

"So he shows up at my dorm room and tells me he's not going, that he can't go because he and Diana had a fight, and he can't leave with her mad and him mad. I told him he was going to the Combine even if it meant I was going to have to tie him to the top of the car and drive him to the airport in Denver tomorrow like that.

"I was like, 'Don, what will happen if you don't go? There's huge repercussions.' That's what he spent the last two years of his life working for. His whole life was geared toward getting to the Combine. They only take 300 of the top athletes in the nation—from any level. For a kid from an NAIA school to get in was something, and now he wasn't going to go?

"I was just dating Stacy—who ended up being my wife —at the time. I sent Stacy over to Diana's to talk about it. Well, of course, we made some progress. I mean, hitting a wall and walking more than a mile in sub-freezing temperature isn't recommended for anyone, much less an athlete who has to be in peak shape to audition for professional coaches and scouts. Had he not gone, he wouldn't have been drafted in the third round—he might not have been drafted at all and ended up just signing as a free agent. Because that's where he ended up opening so many eyes, and then all the attention followed him to Chadron."

Don doesn't like even the memory.

"I can't believe Dan's telling that story," Don said. "But, yes, it's true. And no, I honestly have no idea what the disagreement was about."

"I can tell you this," Dan said. "They never fought again, at least not that I ever heard about. So if they did, I don't know about it. It was unbelievable."

The NFL coaches couldn't believe what they saw in Indianapolis. Beebe ran a 4.39 on the league's slowest turf, which was the best time for any wide receiver there. It was the second best time at the camp behind Deion Sanders, who went 4.29.

"Deion was incredible," Beebe said. "That was the only event he did while he was there. But a 4.29 on that turf is just flying."

Beebe's day started off ominously enough when the tread came off the front half of his shoe.

"I was running and it was just flapping everywhere," Beebe said. "All these guys are there with their agents and $300 shoes, and there I am with my $29 shoes from the discount store. I had to rip the flap off because it looked— and sounded—ridiculous."

Beebe stayed and participated in all the drills. Beebe set a record in the "Four corners run," which involved running forward, sideways, and backward.

No one had ever broken nine seconds in the history of the Combine.

Beebe did. He went 8.9 seconds, best in the Combine that year and ever. He had a vertical jump of 37 inches.

"The whole thing was a different world to me," Beebe

said. "Some of the agents brought girls in for the guys at the motel. I was in a different world, kind of shell-shocked. It was something I had to learn. I just went back to my room at night and called Diana."

The best wide receiver at the Combine that year, according to Beebe, was Andre Rison. "He ran good routes, made good cuts, and caught the ball well," Beebe said. "He just stood out to me more than any receiver."

Rison would end up being a teammate of Beebe's with the Packers during the 1996 Super Bowl season. But back then, Beebe was just hoping to make an impression.

And that, he did.

When Beebe arrived in Chadron after the Combine, the attention started mounting.

"Don got back to Chadron, and Raiders scout Kent McCloughan (a former University of Nebraska football star) and a Green Bay scout were sitting there, waiting on his porch," Giles said.

That was just the start of it. The local biweekly, the *Chadron Record* ran updates on which scouts were visiting.

"After the Combine," Beebe said, "the attention really started. I was getting calls all the time."

Every team in the NFL, except the Denver Broncos and Chicago Bears, contacted Beebe. And 21 NFL teams visited Chadron.

"I thought that was odd," said Chadron State Information Director Con Marshall. "Because Denver is so close (five hours) and Chicago is in his home state."

Diana kept a log of the teams' visits at home.

"We'd mark the team on the calendar and the day they were coming," Diana said. "It was pretty exciting."

"The best part for me was that I got out of class each day," Beebe said, a good student by then. "The scouts would come, and I'd have to miss school to run for them."

The scouts were astounded by both Beebe's skills and Chadron's remoteness.

"The stories the scouts had were funny," Beebe said. "They'd fly to Denver, take a puddle-jumper to Rapid City, rent a car and drive two hours on a two-lane state highway to Chadron."

Not all the scouts were amused.

June Jones, then the offensive coordinator for the Atlanta Falcons, was shocked to get nailed for speeding. "I thought you had to have people to have police cars," Jones said.

Marshall said Jones's fine was $100. "Back then in 1989, a $100 fine was pretty big," Marshall said. "He must've been really speeding, close to 90."

Smith met with all the scouts. They didn't believe Smith when he told them how fast Beebe was.

The New York Jets was the team that showed—from start to finish—the most interest.

"I was sitting across from the scout for the Jets when he came to Chadron," Beebe said.

The scout didn't think Beebe's fledgling legend was real. "Don, I know you're fast, but we'd like to get another time on you," the scout said.

"That's fine," Beebe said. "What if I could run a 4.2 for you?"

The scout gave Beebe a look of disbelief and promised: "Listen, if you run a 4.3, I'll have our offensive coordinator, Rich Kotite, down here to see you," the scout said.

Beebe could tell by the tone in the scout's voice that he wasn't a believer—yet.

"I was like, 'Okay, sucker,'" Beebe recalls. "That lit a little fire under me."

That day, more than any other, anytime, anywhere, Beebe ran like the wind.

"I never felt so fast," Beebe recalls. "It was just something where I was flying on the track. I knew it was 4.2."

Smith stood there, shaking his head.

"The scout kept looking at the time," Smith said. "He looked up, looked at the time, looked down and looked at the time again."

Beebe knew his time, but wanted to hear it from the scout.

"The guy had two clocks and he showed me both, one was a 4.21 and 4.22," Beebe said. "I said, 'Well, I guess you'll send coach Kotite out here.' "

"Kotite will be here," the scout said.

So Kotite came to town not even a week later. But there was a problem. Chadron State quarterback Stewart Perez was nowhere to be found to throw to Beebe. Smith and Kotite couldn't make the tosses required for the patterns Beebe had to run. Don's younger brother, Dan, playing for the Chadron State basketball team at the time, was standing there.

"Don will tell you that I am the worst thrower of all time," Dan said.

"Dan is the worst passer of all time—worse than the worst," Don said.

"Man," Dan said. "That's a little harsh. Hey, they needed someone to throw. I was their only option."

The actual dialogue was even less encouraging for those involved.

"You want me to throw?" Dan asked Don as Smith and Kotite talked.

"Dude, you can't throw, you can't throw at all," Don said.

"I'll do the best I can," Dan said. "Maybe I'll screw up, but I'll try to do the best I can."

"You couldn't throw a spiral to save your life," Don said. "You throw ducks (where the ball wobbles), and ducks are hard to catch, especially when they're low or not on target."

After Kotite mentioned Chadron's close proximity to absolutely nothing ("Gee whiz," Kotite told Smith, "this place is far from who knows where."), Dan started throwing to Don. What happened next is still un-explainable, and might be something for the X-files.

"I promise you, every ball was a spiral," Don recalls. "Every ball was right on the mark. Every ball was perfectly thrown. He could never do it again if he tried. Usually, he was brutal, and threw bad every time. But not that day."

"I had," Dan recalls with a smile, "what they call a career day. Every ball was a fast, tight spiral. I don't know why it was that way. But I knew it was important to him."

Kotite ran Beebe, and verified the sub-4.3-second 40-yard dash times.

"Coach," Kotite told Smith, "this guy is legit."

The Washington Redskins flew Beebe out to check him over. This was another sort of indoctrination as far as what the NFL was about.

"I was answering some questions, and another guy was ahead, in the station ahead of me, and I could hear them," Beebe said. "The (Redskins official) gave the guy some building blocks—you know, the kind you'd give your kids. And he told the player, 'Build something higher than it is wide.' The player was like, 'Higher, like height, or what?' The Redskins official repeated it again, and again, and then told the player he couldn't tell him any more. The guy couldn't build it. He was sitting there, talking to himself, looking so confused that I really felt bad for him. So, I get done with my station, and I go to the blocks."

Beebe remembers the words exchanged as if it were yesterday.

"Please, whatever you do," Beebe told the official, "don't asked me to build something higher than it is wide. Come on, that's insulting."

"I have to," the team official said.

Beebe put one block on top of another.

"There," Beebe said. "It's done."

Buffalo got hot on the trail after the NFL Combine. Bills receivers coach Nick Nicolau came calling as soon as the Jets were done. Nicolau knew little about either Beebe or Chadron.

"The journey was actually longer than that," Nicolau said. "The Bills sent me first to Western Illinois, and I got his background from Western Illinois. The coaches told me about how he wasn't sure what he wanted to do the first time he came there, and then how he worked in siding. They told me how Brad Smith, who used to be an assistant at Western, had gone to Chadron State."

"So after I got done at Western Illinois, I went to Chicago and flew to Denver from there. Then, it was a puddle jumper from Denver to Scottsbluff, and then to Chadron, just flying over the highway like the plane was a car or something—of course, when your attache case is on the wing, you can get a little nervous. I got to Chadron, and of course, there's no rental car place. The pilot, when I got there, asked when I was leaving—see, I was the only stranger on the flight, everyone else knew each other. He asked where I was staying. I told him where I was staying and that I was leaving tomorrow. He picked me up and had coffee. It was really nice."

"I wasn't aware of his times at the Combine," Nicolau said. "Everyone else there was looking for players, but I wasn't employed at the time, so I was looking for a job when I was at the Combine. Don was a complete mystery to me—I knew next to nothing about him, except my new bosses, the Bills, told me to work him out, so that's what I was going to do."

When Nicolau asked about Beebe's speed, Smith didn't know what to say because Smith figured no one would believe Beebe was faster than 4.4.

"I didn't want to tell Nick about the Jets, and the times they got of Beebs," Smith said. "He kept asking me, and I just looked at him and said only, '4.3.'"

Nicolau, his attention caught, looked at Smith. "Oh,

baloney," Nicolau said. "If he runs 4.3 or better, I'll pack him in my suitcase and take him home with me now."

At that point, Smith wasn't sure Nicolau trusted him any more. Beebe warmed up for only five minutes before announcing he was ready.

"Nick said most guys take 20 minutes to stretch," Smith said. "I just kind of shrugged my shoulders."

Beebe ran another 4.22. Nicolau just stared at the watch. Then, a 4.3. And finally, another 4.28.

"I can't take this back to Buffalo," Nicolau said. "They won't believe me. There's no way someone from Chadron, Nebraska could be this fast."

Nicolau figured Smith had just measured the 40 yards short by a few feet—or yards. So the two went and got a measuring tape.

How close to 40 yards was it?

"Forty yards," Smith said. "Right on the beak."

"I worked him out indoors," Nicolau recalls. "He ran a 4.2-something. Now, I'm not a professional timer, so I had him run again, and he goes like 4.3. I went back to the Bills and wrote Don up real well, that I liked what I saw, and what kind of person he is. You know that as a coach, you're going to work with the guys you pick six hours a day, so you don't want a guy you won't like or can't teach."

Nicolau reported to John Butler, director of player personnel, and Buffalo's general manager at the time, Bill Polian.

"Obviously after the Combine, it got to the point where Don was far from being an unknown," Polian said. "Chadron isn't a household name, and it was, at that time, off the beaten path on the football map, but he had put some good numbers there. Really, when you have real 4.2 time, you don't stay unknown. And Don really was a 4.2. From what I hear today, he still is."

With the Draft still a couple of months away, Buffalo, without a pick in the first or second round, already knew who it wanted with its first pick of the draft, which was in the third round.

"We were already pretty serious about Don when we sent Nick out there," said Butler, now the Buffalo Bills' general manager. "Nick was the position (wide receivers) coach. But, yes, Nick's trip pretty much solidified that if Don was still there in the third round, we wanted him."

ESPN did a feature on Beebe and Millikin College's Jeff Query, who ironically ended up being drafted by the Green Bay Packers. Both were fast and from small colleges. ESPN called the feature "Speed on the Prairie." By then, at least for NFL scouts and coaches, Beebe was basically a household name.

Don and Diana with Bill Giles, the NFL scout who
brought Don to the attention of the NFL Combine.

The ESPN camera crew taping Don at Chadron State prior to the NFL Draft in 1989.

Celebrating a big moment. Don and Diana celebrate with his mom and dad and Chadron State football coach Brad Smith after Don is drafted by the Buffalo Bills in 1989.

12

NEXT STOP:
THE NFL AND BUFFALO

The Beebes had 21 family members and friends to their small "mother-in-law" house in Chadron for the NFL Draft in May, 1989.

Up until almost right before the Draft, Don had yet to pick an agent. With little interest in hooking up with some of the agents he had either seen or heard about, a friend, Kay Erickson told Don she knew of a man in northern California who represented some West Coast-based players. Don soon talked to Bob LaMonte and signed up to be a client.

"When a guy calls, says he's 5-foot-10, 175 pounds and played one year at Chadron State in Nebraska, which I hadn't heard of up to that point, it doesn't exactly make your day," said LaMonte. "Then I saw his times, and they were good. But everyone's a 4.2—only that really means they're about a 4.4 to 4.5. But Don really was a 4.2."

Beebe did not know where he'd be drafted, but the news became more encouraging by the day.

"I still, at that point, was thinking I'd probably go later rather than sooner, although the Combine had been encouraging," Don said. "But Bob talked to some scouts, and he figured I'd go from the second to fourth rounds."

The family had gone all out for the day. A cake was made at a Chadron bakery with the NFL logo on it. And Don's mother made a flag out of construction paper with each NFL team on it. At the time, the Beebes were pretty much convinced that the New York Jets would draft Don. San Francisco, Tampa Bay, and the Bills all seemed possible, as well as the Raiders or the Kansas City Chiefs, who had sent former all-Pro receiver Otis Taylor to Chadron to work out with Beebe.

"We were all anxious about getting a phone call," Beebe said. "The house was just packed, jam packed."

Beebe remembered how, over the years, he had watched players during the Draft, and how frustrated they would be, especially if they did not get drafted as high as they were projected, or expected, to go.

"I had heard guys saying stuff like, 'Draft day was the worst day of my life,'" Beebe said. "It wasn't that way for me at all. I had Diana and my family there, and some close friends. With or without the Draft, that's a perfect day for me."

While going higher, rather than lower, in the Draft

would be nice, Beebe did not stress when he did not hear his name in the first two rounds.

"It got toward the end of the day," Beebe said. "I was not worried about it. I really wasn't panicked. What was going to happen would happen. The Lord was in control."

But which team did Beebe prefer?

"Tampa Bay would have been nice," Beebe said. "Diana liked that, and we wanted to get out of the cold."

Well, at 5:00 p.m., the little house behind the big house in Chadron, Nebraska was still full of people. And the only phone calls were well-wishers and others wanting to know if Don had heard anything yet.

"At five, ESPN's Draft coverage ended for that day," Beebe said. "They had gotten to the start of the third round, but the coverage was scheduled to, and did, stop at 5:00 p.m., I was still in a good mood, but there was a little anticipation and a letdown. We started to wind things down a little bit. I understood at that point that we'd find something out the next day."

Things wound up in a hurry. The phone rang at 5:07 p.m., just 420 seconds from the time ESPN went off the air. The Draft was still going on, and would continue Sunday as well with the final of the 12 rounds.

"I always thought it would be the Jets," Beebe said. "I ran a 4.21, and they brought out Richie Kotite, their offensive coordinator, and they only do that when they're serious. And when ESPN went off the air, the Jets had a pick coming up about then. So I was convinced I was going to New York."

Well, he was going to New York, just a little further

west than he had planned.

"It was the guy who was at the Draft for Buffalo," Don said.

"Is this Don Beebe," the Bills official asked.

"Yes, it is," he said.

"Don, I'm just calling to inform you that the Buffalo Bills have taken you with their first pick of the Draft, in the third round, the 82nd pick overall," the official said.

"Thanks," Don said. "It's nice to be part of your organization."

At that point, the house erupted. Chadron State coach Brad Smith had walked home, just a few blocks away, midway through the second round. He was walking back at 5 p.m. when ESPN's draft coverage concluded to let Don know that Smith was sure Don would be drafted early Sunday.

"You just heard this explosion of yelling and screaming," Smith said. "I started running to their house because I knew he'd gotten the call and been drafted."

But to those in the house, the question was which team had drafted Don. He had not uttered "Buffalo" or "Bills" or any other team for that matter. Everyone in the room was trying to prompt Don, who was in deep thought listening to the team official on the phone, who was explaining details of Don's upcoming trip to Buffalo to meet team officials and the media.

People in the room at the small house started holding up signs. Tampa's flag was held up, Don shook his head no, and then turned to concentrate on what the official was saying. He turned again, and someone held up the Raiders flag. Don waved his hand, indicating no, it wasn't the Raiders. Up came the Jets flag. No, Don motioned. Down with the Jets flag.

The official gave Beebe the name Nina, a secretary with whom Beebe was supposed to speak and then meet at the airport. Don motioned for paper and a pen. He scribbled "Nin" and blotched the "a"—both from hurrying while he was writing and the pen's felt tip. Someone leaned over and saw the "Nin" and mistook the "a" for an "e". Assuming Don had just forgotten the last letter, they figured he had written "Niners." His friends from California were ecstatic, for they believed Don had just been drafted by the Niners. Again, Don heard the commotion, as everyone celebrated the drafting of Don Beebe by the San Francisco 49ers.

By now, Beebe had gotten his wits about himself, and was talking to Bills head coach Marv Levy.

"Don, we're glad you were there in the third round," Levy said. "You were the player we wanted."

"Thanks, coach," Don said. "Diana and I are looking forward to seeing you in Buffalo."

Beebe was joining one of the strongest up-and-coming franchises in the AFC with one of the best quarterbacks, Jim Kelly.

The Bills did not have a pick in the first or second rounds because of a trade that brought Cornelius Bennett to Buffalo. That trade also involved Eric Dickerson and Greg Bell, in addition to draft picks.

"Our scouts liked him," Bills coach Marv Levy said. "I watched him workout at the combine. I was impressed with his speed and athleticism."

The Bills needed some speed, and found it in an oasis on the Nebraska prairie.

"Before the Draft, the Bills people asked me, 'Do you think he's worth a third round pick?'" said Nick Nicolau, the Bills' receivers coach at the time. "I was up in my office, not in the war room. There was a wide receiver from Duke and another from North Carolina State on the board when we made our first pick, which was the third-rounder. They come running up, and someone asks me, 'Beebe's still there, what do we do?' I said, 'Take him, someone else didn't do their homework if that guy is still there.' When a guy plays at a small college, you wonder how they compare to guys at a major college. But Don had that one magic ingredient—speed. To make it as a receiver, you have to have speed. So we worked Don into our three-receiver set with James Lofton on one side, Beebe on the other, and Andre Reed in the middle. It was like, 'Pick your poison' when we lined up. Know what I mean?"

Buffalo knew what it was getting in Beebe.

"We did a lot of research on Don," said Carolina general manager Bill Polian, who was Buffalo's GM at the time. "We knew he was the kind of person we wanted on our football team."

"I was on the phone a good 20 minutes," Beebe said. "Everyone was saying, 'Who is it, who is it?' But I'm talking to Marv Levy by now, so what could I do? Marv said he was glad I was there, that they felt lucky to get me. He reassured me, said he couldn't wait to see me when I got in. So I got off the phone, and it was hysteria."

Buffalo!

Finally, the 21 people in a house that was built for less than a quarter of that number erupted one final time. Don Beebe was going to join the Buffalo Bills. No warm weather, but a good team with a great coach in Levy, and one of the best quarterbacks in the NFL, Kelly, who threw the ball as much as almost any quarterback in the league.

KDUH-TV, the local ABC affiliate in Scottsbluff, Nebraska, the hub for western Nebraska and the closest shopping mall to Chadron, located 100 miles south in the panhandle, was also at Beebe's house.

"KDUH came up with their camera and did a big interview in the backyard," Beebe said. "Everyone was really having a good time."

From the first fall camp at Western Illinois, some six years earlier, to a season of college basketball, to a junior college, back to Western Illinois and all the questions about eligibility, to Chadron, Nebraska, a spot heretofore unknown on the maps of NFL scouts—Beebe's journey, just to that point, had been incredible.

"I look back, and if this isn't the Lord's handprints all over it, then what is it?" Beebe said. "I mean, come on, you have a guy who played two years of college football, one at Western Illinois and one at Chadron. And a couple of years later, he's a team's first pick of the Draft. What more would it take to convince you?"

Throw in the marriage, the fact that Dan walked on at Chadron State and was about to earn a scholarship for basketball, and, well, it was quite a time.

"That," Don said, "was a fun semester."

Diana and Don flew to Buffalo to meet the coaches and the Buffalo media.

"That was another shellshock," Don said.

Worried about taking Diana into that environment, Don was concerned. However, destiny left another handprint.

On the day the Beebes flew into Buffalo, Alexander Mogilny was defecting from Russia to play for the Buffalo Sabres in the NHL.

"So we didn't get all the media attention, and that was nice," Diana said. "It really took a lot of the attention away from us, and we were happy about that."

Don couldn't believe the coincidence. "He landed within probably the same 15-minute time frame that we did," Beebe said, shaking his head at the irony. "Sure, I was part of a story, the top pick of Buffalo. But Alexander, that is a huge story, not just locally, but nationally and internationally."

Don has a pre-Draft workout with Buffalo Bills receivers coach, Nick Nicolau, who would be Don's coach for three years in Buffalo.

Don and June Jones, then a scout and later head coach of the Atlanta Falcons, just prior to the 1989 NFL Draft.

Don and Otis Taylor, former All-Pro receiver with the Kansas City Chiefs, prior to the 1989 NFL Draft.

13

No Time for the Pain

ever previously hurt at any level of competition, the injury bug plagued Beebe in Buffalo.

"The third day of camp, I pulled a hamstring," Beebe said. "It was the first injury I had in any sport."

His time in Buffalo wasn't all spent on the shelf. Far from it.

Beebe's first catch was as memorable as they come. In the 1989 season, with Buffalo involved in the equivalent of an old fashioned gridiron shootout with Houston—a team it would have another unforgetable game with a couple of years later in the playoffs—Beebe hauled in his first NFL catch. It was a 63-yard bomb from quarterback Jim Kelly for a touchdown, helping push the Bills to a 47-41 win in overtime.

During the season, Don reinjured the hamstring. Again,

he came back in a loud way. And it wasn't an easy way to do it either. Because in the Playoffs on January 6, 1990, against Cleveland, Beebe made his first highlight video. Earlier in that game, Beebe was upended and had his head torpedoed into the ground, spraining his neck. He came back and made a crucial catch on fourth down and 10 to keep the game's final drive alive, although the Bills ultimately fell short.

"When Don took that hit, I thought he was dead," said Nick Nicolau, the Bills' receivers coach at the time. "You look at receivers and think, just by the nature of the position, that they are not tough guys. That showed how tough Don is."

Beebe finished his rookie season with 17 catches for 317 yards and two touchdowns in the regular season. Twice he had four receptions in a game, in road games at Indianapolis (Oct. 8) and at New England (Nov. 19). Beebe also returned kickoffs, averaging 22.1 yards on 16 returns. Included in that was an 85-yarder in the closing minutes of a tight game against Atlanta (Nov. 5).

During his second year, the 1990 season, Beebe played in 12 games, while suffering the worst injury of his career. He also started four games.

On December 23, 1990, Beebe was enjoying his best day of the season, with three catches for 74 yards against Miami. And that was coming off a huge 17-13 win over the New York Giants the week before when he caught a 43-yard touchdown pass from Frank Reich in the second half to key the win. So he was excited playing Miami two days before Christmas.

"I'll never forget that day," Beebe said.

Neither will the 80,000 who were watching the game at Rich Stadium. Beebe was blocking Miami defensive back Tim McKyer.

"We were running a sweep my way," Beebe said.

Bills running back Thurman Thomas cut underneath Beebe's block. Miami linebacker John Offerdahl was "scraping" along the line of scrimmage in a lateral pursuit to cut Thomas off when he turned upfield.

"As Thurman cut up the field, John dove at him," Beebe said. "But he missed."

He missed Thomas, but got Beebe—all of Beebe.

"He hit the side of my leg," Beebe said, "and I felt my leg split in half."

Offerdahl had broken Beebe's fibula and tibia.

"He was doing his job on that play—he got hurt on a blocking assignment," said Nicolau. "I always marvel how different athletes come back, or don't come back, from serious injuries. Don came back. I know his strong religious beliefs really helped him through that time."

There was little doubt in Beebe's mind that the injury was extraordinarily serious.

"As I rolled over on the field," Beebe said. "I brought my left leg over my body and saw it flop on the turf. I thought my career was over. I thought, 'No, it can't be over, it's just my second year.' And I was having a really good season."

Beebe's best friend, Frank Reich, was playing quarterback for the Bills. He saw what happened to Beebe, and ran to his side. "Give it to the Lord, Don," Reich said as Beebe squirmed in excruciating pain. "Let's give it to the Lord now."

Beebe said he'll never forget that moment, or what happened afterward.

"We prayed in front of 80,000 people in that stadium," Don said. "I felt no pain from that point on until I was off the field. The prayer numbed it for a while."

Fans who saw the grotesque way Beebe's left leg bounced on the turf when he rolled over were shocked to see him smile as he went off the field on a cart.

"Don is one of the toughest players we ever had," said Bill Polian, the former Buffalo general manager. "He never gave up—always worked hard."

Beebe was waving to the fans and smiling as they cheered his last name, "Bee-be, Bee-be."

"After that, people would ask how I could break my leg that badly, get up in the cart, and smile as I waved to the crowd—and by waving I was telling them that I wasn't done, I would be back," Beebe said. "It's because I have Jesus Christ in my life."

Mentally, the injury stung as much as the physical pain."

"That injury was real tough for me to handle," Beebe said. "Because I knew we had a shot at going to the Playoffs and the Super Bowl."

Still, Beebe didn't let the injury get him down.

"I knew I'd be back and we'd use this in the positive way," Beebe said. "Look at the (game) tape—everyone's cheering my name as I leave the field. I knew I'd be back."

As Beebe was carted off the field, the pain came back.

"The pain was intense," Beebe said. "They had to numb it completely. The doctor took out a needle that was 8 to 10 inches long. The doctor said before he pushed the needle in my shin, 'This is the most pain you will ever feel.'"

The doctor was right.

"It was like fire in my leg," Beebe said. "The doctor said, 'You might want to bite a towel or something.' So I did. They wanted to do surgery right then. But I wanted to be with my family on Christmas. I was on the couch and everyone was there, my whole family. The pain just got to be too much. The pain was getting worse and worse—unbearable. I called the doctor at midnight on Christmas Eve. I was losing the color in my foot. An intern came over and cut the cast and I got the color back. But the pressure was on top now, on the broken bone, because of the weight of the cast. A few hours later I called the doctor and said, 'Call an ambulance, I can't take this.'"

Surgery came early the next morning on Christmas Day.

"The day after surgery, I was laying there in the hospital, and a nurse came in," Beebe said. "She said, 'The little girl next door is a fan of Don Beebe and the Bills. She has spinal cancer, and we don't know how long she will live.' She was 12 years old. She came into the room in a wheelchair."

Melissa Stanton entered Don's room—and his life. Had he had surgery the first night, and gotten out of the hospital the next day, he never would have met Melissa. He's glad he did.

"We hit it off right away—she's just a great kid," Beebe said. "She was such an inspiration to me. I saw her, and she looked up at me. She said, 'Don't worry, Don, you'll be all right.' I thought, 'What a strong kid. All I have is a broken leg. Look at what she's dealing with.' And she was the one consoling me, telling me everything would be all right. She has been such an inspiration to me."

That made Beebe feel that the broken leg, the decision to delay going to the hospital, then speeding it up Christmas Eve, was meant to be.

"We've been friends ever since," Don said. "People wonder why tragedies happen. But if this wouldn't have happened, I wouldn't have met Melissa. I can't imagine life without Melissa. She's had so many surgeries. Her heart has stopped several times. But she keeps making it. To this day, she's doing great. She's been uplifting to me, to tell the truth. God used me to touch her life, and she touched my life."

A benefit Beebe organized helped get Melissa through some tough times, and the pair remain fast friends today, making the best of a what was potentially a bad situation for anyone else.

What was really bad for Beebe was the rehabilitation. At least, it was tough for the family to watch during the family's annual vacation in Minnesota. With a rod installed in his leg—which he carries to this day—Beebe set about not just getting the leg back to where it was, but making it even stronger.

"He's hopping up this hill just on his bad leg, his left leg, again and again and again," his sister Beth recalls. "Sweating, the pain so bad, it made us cry just to watch him. But he never quit."

Don knew at that point that he would be stronger.

"Our trainer, Bud Carpenter, said, 'Once you have the okay, you can do as much as you want and you can't hurt the leg or anything,'" Don said. "Well, I had the okay. It was time to get to work. My brothers and my family helped push me so hard. I will never forget that"

Back in Illinois, the rehab continued.

"I ran on sandhills in the Illinois area, a steep sandhill," Don said. "No one could get up it, not even my brother David, and he's a good athlete. He was puking. I was running sets up it."

"I was so proud of him," David said. "You had to see it to actually understand what he was doing, the power of his spirit."

"On the steep hill, I kept running, pounding and pounding on the one leg," Don said. "I'd go until I literally couldn't do it any more. I remember once, in the pouring rain, I fell down the hill. I just laid there for a while, because no one could see me. But I got up, and kept going. That rod is still in my leg. It doesn't bother me, I can't even tell its there. There are some guys who have had this injury, like Joe Theisman. His bone came out of the skin. I had a thin layer of skin left, but you could still see the bone. It was tough."

Just like the rehab.

"God instilled in me, through my parents, the work ethic," Don said. "If I still wanted to play in this league, I'd have to work at it."

He also worked on his hands.

"My second year in the league, I had a couple of games

where I dropped some balls, and it really affected me," Beebe said. "I wanted to correct it. Every day, I'd catch hundreds of balls out of the 'jugs' machine."

He'd have his mother, brother or sisters run the machine.

"He'd decide he was going to catch 50 or 100 balls in a row, and if he dropped one, he'd get so mad at himself," David said.

"Yep, he'd come over say, 'Set it up again!'" Beth recalled. "The perfect practice made almost perfect."

"It got to the point where I could stand right next to the machine and catch the ball coming out at 50 miles an hour," Beebe said. He reached the point where he knew he could catch anything. That, as much as the practice itself, helped.

"It's all a mental thing," Don said. "If you say you can't do it, you probably won't—whether it's sports or not. I said I was going to catch balls, so I did."

The 1991 season could not have started any better. Beebe was experiencing another fire, only this one had nothing to do with a needle in his shin. Rather, he was a thorn in the side of opponents.

"That was a bad injury," Polian said. "But I will tell you this, that when he came back, he was at least as fast as he was before."

On September 8, Beebe tied a Bills record with four touchdown receptions against Pittsburgh, catching 10 passes that game for 112 yards, marking the first 100-receiving yards day in his career.

"That year, the Lord blessed me early in the season," Beebe said. "In the first game, I had almost 100 yards versus Miami. In the second game, I had four touchdowns and 10 catches against the Steelers. So I started off the next season strong.

"I'll never forget that night after the Steeler game. I was watching Chris Berman on ESPN's *NFL Prime Time*. They were showing the tape of me getting carried off the field in the Miami game from the year before when I broke my leg. Berman said, 'All you people who doubted Don Beebe, thought his career was over—NOT! He had four touchdowns today against Pittsburgh.' That was great. In a six-month period, I was brand new again. I still had some pain and swelling, but I was faster than ever."

Beebe had seven starts in the first 11 games, catching 32 passes for 414 yards. With five games left in the season, he was on pace to break 50 receptions for the first time.

But another break came first, and it had to do with not a catch, rather, but catching a bad break. On November 18, Beebe broke his collarbone against Miami.

"That year, I was in the top three in the league in several categories after three or four games," Don said. "I had, like, 23 catches and four touchdowns."

But the injury curbed that.

"I looked at the calendar when they said how long I would be out," Beebe said. "If we made the Playoffs, my season wasn't over."

The Bills made the Playoffs, and Beebe's fire burned again, picking up where he left off and then some. He tied for the postseason team lead in receptions with James Lofton and Andre Reed with 11 catches. Those catches went for 221 yards and a career-high 20.1 average. Although the Bills lost their second Super Bowl later that month, Beebe did pick up his first Super Bowl touchdown catch during the 37-24 loss to the Washington Redskins.

The following season, 1992, was Beebe's finest to that point, and was the second of four seasons in which he caught at least 30 passes. Once again, however, the injury bug found him just below the neck. He missed the first four games on the injured reserve list with a hamstring pull. However, he came back to start eight of the 12 games he played, and led all Bills receivers with four 100-yard games. In his first game back from the injury, he caught six passes for 106 yards against the Jets (Oct. 26). He followed that two weeks later with a season-high eight catches for 101 yards against the Steelers including a season longest 65-yard touchdown at Indianapolis (Nov. 29). Against Denver the second week in December, Beebe had a 64-yard touchdown catch among his four catches for 104 yards.

Beebe played in all four of Buffalo's postseason games that year, including the 52-17 loss to Dallas in the Super Bowl, and made the play where he tracked down Leon Lett to secure both players' places in Super Bowl lore.

In 1993, he had another good season, despite separating his shoulder in training camp. That only slowed, not stopped, Beebe. He still caught 31 passes. That season was also a career-best in terms of starts with 14. He also became just the 13th receiver in Bills history to pass the 2,000-receiving yards plateau and the 27th to catch at least 100 passes as a Bill.

Beebe's 31 catches were fifth best on the team, with 504

yards and three touchdowns. The best game of the year for Beebe came against the Raiders when he caught just four passes but had 115 receiving yards, including a 65-yard touchdown reception. His hustle showed no signs of dissipating as he received a game ball for jumping on a fumble late in the fourth quarter against the New York Giants on November 15 to allow what turned out to be the game winning drive to continue.

However, Beebe did miss a pair of games in the middle of the season because of a hamstring injury. Still, he had arguably his best Super Bowl in the second consecutive Super Bowl defeat at the hands of the repeating-champion Dallas Cowboys, who won, 30-13.

Beebe had no idea he was saving his best for last, but that's exactly what ended up happening during the 1994 season, which would be his final one in Buffalo. He caught a career-high 40 passes for what was, to that point, a career-best 527 yards. Of the 13 games he played in that season, he started 11. An October 16 game against the Colts ended up being a day of milestones for Beebe. He passed the 1,000 mark in return yards and the 2,200 mark in receiving yards.

"Don had a lot of big games," Polian said. "The bigger the game, it seemed, the better Don was. And he was always a magnificent individual."

A concussion three weeks later against the New York Jets forced Beebe to miss three games. Again, his return was quite an occasion.

In Miami, a place memorable for several reasons during his career, Beebe burned the Dolphins for a 72-yard touchdown catch from Jim Kelly, among the three passes for 89 yards he caught that day.

In a rematch three weeks later (Dec. 24) with the Colts, Beebe had a season-high eight catches for 111 yards, his seventh career 100-yard receiving game.

With expansion teams Jacksonville and Carolina coming, the Bills had some tough choices to make, not signing either Beebe, Frank Reich or tight end Pete Metzelaars to contracts.

Don Beebe's career with the Bills had come to an end.

Beebe still wishes he wouldn't have missed so many games because of injuries.

"If I could get one thing back, and I know those things happened for a reason, but if I could change one thing, it would've been that I played a whole season healthy in Buffalo," Beebe said.

"It's one of the great organizations in pro sports," Beebe said. "Marv Levy; Nick Nicolau; Charlie Joiner (who succeeded Nicolau as wide receivers coach); the general manager at the time, Bill Polian; and (future GM in Buffalo) John Butler were just the best to me. I really wish I could've seen what I could have done."

To this day, Polian and Butler said Beebe's time in Buffalo was well spent.

"He came back from tough, tough injuries," Butler said. "He had great ability and great dignity. The kind of person he is, he has few peers. Not only was he an outstanding player, he was an outstanding person in every phase. I'd like to see every player be like Don Beebe."

"We never regretted drafting Don," Polian said. "He

was a huge part of the success we had there. You never turn down the chance to get a Don Beebe."

Beebe said the injuries, on the one hand, cost him time—game time. On the other hand, it gave him time to spend with his family.

"I look back, and that was just the Lord's way for me," Beebe said. "He didn't want me at that level, a Pro Bowl kind of guy. I look back now, and I'm content with it. When you're at the Pro Bowl level, it's more pressing on your family time, and your family is in the limelight. And that, I wouldn't want. I love my family, and I'm a private person. I don't want them in the limelight. I'm a homebody, and at that level, it's tough to be that way."

To this day, Polian, now the general manager for the Carolina Panthers, almost glows when he talks about Beebe and the Bills' team Polian helped build.

"What Don and those guys did was so special, they were all so close, like a family. Even today when I see them at weddings or other events, it's just such a warm feeling because we all care about each other so much, and always will," Polian said. "These weren't guys who showboated, or who ripped their helmets off when they made a good play to be seen on television. Marv (Levy) used to say, 'What you do speaks so loudly, I can't hear what you are saying.' That was this team. No nicknames, no bad image, no one was flamboyant. Just a bunch of guys who cared about each other—and went to four Super Bowls. These guys would come down the tunnel after games and give high-fives to stadium workers, anyone. I look at Don and the guys we had then, and boy, that was a special bunch."

After breaking his leg on December 23, 1990 vs. Miami, Don raised his fist in determination to let the Buffalo fans know he would be back the following year.

Don's roommate on the road with Buffalo, Frank Reich, and his wife Linda. Two of the Beebe's best friends.

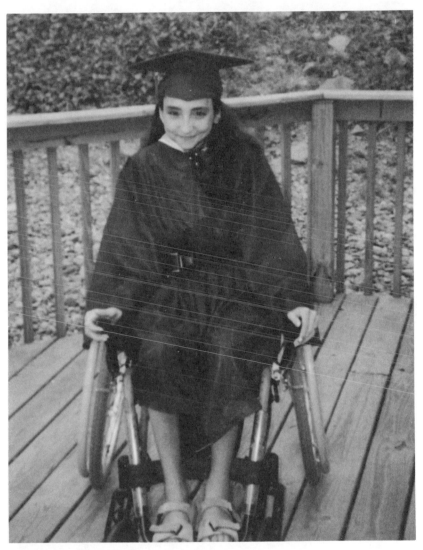

Melissa Stanton, the little girl that I met in the hospital in Buffalo when I broke my leg. She has truly been an inspiration to me. She has fought cancer of the spine much of her life. She recently graduated from high school.

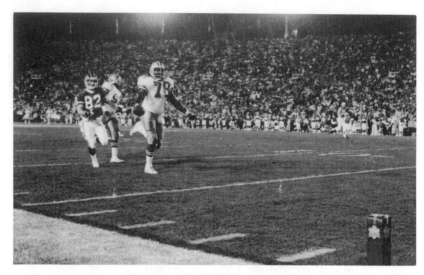

Don chases down Leon Lett of the Dallas Cowboys in Super Bowl XXVII. In the next fraction of a second, Don knocked the ball from Lett's hand to prevent the Cowboys from scoring another touchdown on the Bills.

Don landing on his head in the 1990 Playoffs. "I'm still wondering how I survived that one."

14

THE LEON LETT PLAY

ame for Don Beebe became infamy for Leon Lett, despite the fact that the Cowboys slammed the Bills, 52-17, in Super Bowl XXVII in January, 1993.

Late in the game—the most watched sports event on television—Lett picked up a fumble by Bills backup quarterback Frank Reich. Lett, a 6-foot-6, 290-pound defensive end, ran 64 yards with it. The final 10 or so yards, Lett started holding the ball out to his right side, almost down to his knee, giving the appearance of showboating.

Beebe, on the other hand, had nothing but business on his mind. Having sprinted from the opposite end of the field the moment Beebe saw Reich fumble, Beebe caught Lett inside the one yard line, swatting the ball away and out of the end zone for a touch back. That gave the Bills the ball and preserved the final score and margin, much to the delight—or chagrin—of bettors, who wager on the point spread and even the numbers in the score.

"I didn't think anything of it," Beebe said. "I saw the ball was fumbled, and a guy picked it up. It was my job to tackle him. I don't care if some guy from Vegas had $40,000 riding on it. I sprinted down the field because that's what I'm supposed to do."

The play the Bills ran on the fumble was designed to get Beebe as far down field as possible.

"I was running a fly pattern down the left side of the field," Beebe recalls. "When I turned and looked, I saw Frank scrambling a little bit. I kind of slowed down, and I was trying to get in a position where he could hit me with the ball."

Reich didn't see an open receiver, and the Dallas rush, as it had been all game, was closing fast.

"I was at least 40 yards away from Frank," Beebe said. "I started working my way back. He fumbled. The ball was picked up right away by Leon Lett. When I saw him pick up the ball, I saw him run down the field. I was sprinting. I thought I was going to get him. By the time he got to the 10, I was passing the 15. I thought I'd get him. I never doubted that I'd catch him."

But what would the 5-11, 185-pound Beebe do if he caught Lett? Judging by the size differential, perhaps just a good scolding for Lett's showboating was in order.

"With about 20 yards left, I was thinking, 'How am I going to do this?'" Beebe said. "I mean, I'm thinking, 'This guy is HUGE!' To tell you the truth, I was going to jump on his back."

Then, Lett started showing off, holding the ball out.

"Unfortunately for him, he put it out there and gave me the opportunity to slap it away," Beebe said. "People saw it as a great act of hustle. But I don't take credit for that. That goes to my parents, they brought me up with the right morals, values, and work ethic."

A lot of fans thought Lett deserved the humiliation just for showing off and holding the ball out.

"People sometimes say, 'I'm glad you shut him up,'" Beebe said. "I look at it in a different way. Here's a defensive lineman picking up a football, a guy who has probably never scored a touchdown in his life. He knows he's going to score. He's sure he's going to score. I don't believe Leon was trying to rub it in. He was just excited. It was just unfortunate for him that this little pipsqueak was there to knock it away."

At the end of the play, Beebe didn't celebrate. He tore his helmet off in disgust and jogged to the sideline.

"What was there to celebrate?" Beebe said. "We were getting beaten badly."

Even heading off the field, Beebe didn't know he'd done something as special as it turned out to be.

"At first, it didn't mean anything," Beebe said. "We got the ball back at the 20, and we wanted to score. The first time it meant anything to me was after the game. I was sitting in front of my locker and I'm upset we lost. All the guys were totally defeated. But then, the Bills' owner, Ralph Wilson, walked by my locker, shook my hand, looked me square in the face. He said, 'Son, you showed me a lot today. That meant a lot to me, that a guy like you can represent the Buffalo Bills like that. Thank you.' I was like, wow, Mr. Wilson said that. I thought, 'Man I did do something pretty good.'"

John Butler, now Buffalo's general manager, was the Bills' director of pro player personnel that year and when the Bills drafted Beebe in 1989.

"That play exemplified what any organization wants to see from its players," Butler said. "We were losing, but Don Beebe is not the kind who would ever quit. That play just shows the kind of person Don is. It's the perfect play for him to be remembered by, because that's what he stands for. He's got the great speed, obviously, and he wouldn't have made the play without that speed. But does anyone else in the NFL make that play beside Don Beebe? No. It's a one-of-a-kind play from a one-of-a-kind player."

Bill Polian, the former Bills general manager, said he still hears about the play.

"To me, that play described Don better than anything anyone could ever say or write about him," Polian said. "Another NFL head coach, who I know very well, told me, 'That's the most unique play I've ever seen—the Super Bowl is over, you've lost, and there comes Beebe.' That's Don. You couldn't find 10 players in the NFL who could have, or would have, made that play. The Super Bowl was a lopsided loss for us that year, but people remember something very positive about the Buffalo Bills because of Don's play."

ABC sportscaster Dick Schaap, who wrote *Return to Glory*, a book about the Green Bay Packers' 1996 Super

Bowl season, of which Beebe was a part, said Beebe's place in football history is secure.

"The part of that play that attracts the public is that Don never quit," Schaap said. "That was one of the great plays in the history of football. Buffalo was losing, and most any player from any team would've thought that there was no reason to kill yourself because the game was so far out of reach."

Reich, Beebe's best friend, said the play just typifies who Beebe is.

"Certainly, it's a defining moment in Don's career that speaks volumes about the kind of person he is," Reich said. "I don't care what you say, unless you have the kind of character a person like Don has, you don't make those plays. It's not a matter of it being something you just turn on and say, 'Okay, it's the Super Bowl, it's time to make a play.' It's who you are and what you stand for.'"

Of course, Reich couldn't let it end there.

"I could've caught Leon," Reich said with a smile. "But it would have looked bad if I would have gotten up and had to run past Don to get Leon."

When it's pointed out that Reich, who entered the 1997 season playing for the Detroit Lions, doesn't have sprinter's speed, he concedes, again with a grin, that maybe Beebe was the one chosen to make the play.

"I'll do anything to make Don look good," Reich said, by now in full laugh. "Don got all the notoriety because of that play. But if it wasn't for me fumbling that ball, the history of the Super Bowl is different, and they have to find another highlight to show the million times a year they show Don's play on Leon. I'll go to any length to make Don look good, even if it means I have to fumble in the Super Bowl."

Beebe and Reich have that kind of relationship, and it's hard to tell who enjoys it more. At the same time, even Beebe wasn't ready for the onslaught of mail and publicity —which continues to this day—about that Super Bowl moment for the ages.

"The letters—at first just the volume of letters—was unbelievable," Beebe said. "The ones what touched me the most were the fathers."

Like this one, which reads, in part:

> *I've never been able to reach my son. We never had a great relationship. Then I see this play where you don't give up. I show my son the play, and say this is how you act in sports, and in life. Our relationship has changed because of it. You'll never understand how much your action meant to a lot of people. Thank you.*

"I think of that and it's like, wow, did the Lord use that or what," Beebe said. "You could tell the guy was emotional when he wrote it—I was crying when I read it. That's what I'm in football for, to touch people's lives. It's touching to read these letters, because you never know who's watching. You never know when the Lord's going to use you to touch people's lives."

"I never knew that moment would come in Super Bowl XXVII," Beebe said. "But then you look back, and it just had to be Super Bowl XXVII. If it was a regular season game, they would have shown it on ESPN; a good play, but, really, not that big of a deal. But no, it is in a Super Bowl, and now it's one of the greatest moments in Super Bowl history, and it's on videos as one of the top plays in the Super Bowl."

The hate mail Lett received from gamblers bothers Beebe to this day.

"A lot of folks wrote Leon or me and said we cost them a lot of money," Beebe said. "To tell you the truth, I don't care about that. I could care less. But one guy sent me something. It was the next year in the playoffs, the AFC Championship game against Kansas City. I go into the locker room and see this long box in my locker. It was open—obviously Frank opened it. He said, 'Looked like a golf club, Don; had to open it up. It's a putter.' This guy sends me a rock putter made out of Arizona rock, very unique."

Enclosed with this note:

Don, just wanted to thank you with all my heart. Was unemployed, didn't have much money, gambled the few thousand I did have (on the Super Bowl). You won me a lot of money. In turn, I started making putters. In a year's time, my business has now flourished and I'm doing great. I just wanted to send you one of the first ones I ever made.

"I still have the putter," Beebe said. "I don't support

that as a way of getting back on your feet, and I hope he doesn't gamble it away. But it's good that he was able to start his own business and get headed in the right direction again. It was a pretty happy story."

Beebe's legacy, even with another good season, a sixth Super Bowl appearance or a second Super Bowl victory will always be inextricably intertwined with the Lett play.

That's fine with Beebe.

"People say, 'What's it like to be known for that and not known for catching a game-winning touchdown pass?'" Beebe said. "I look at it a different way. Ninety-nine percent of the guys who go out of this league, when they're gone a few years down the road, you don't know who they are anymore. Of the one percent that's left, half of that percent is known for a negative thing—wife abuse, drug abuse, something bad. The other half of that percent is what I fall into, someone who touched people's lives in a positive way."

"So when I'm 60 years old, people will remember me from Super Bowl XXVII. It's good to be known for a positive thing."

The whole premise for the play, as spectacular as it turned out, with Beebe zooming down the field, closing in on the hapless Lett and knocking the ball away to keep the score at 52-17, was actually quite fundamental: hard work.

"When I speak to groups, which I really enjoy doing, I tell the kids, 'Never give up,'" Beebe said. "But it's more important that the Lord uses this to touch the parents. In the course of the game, when I see the ball fumbled and Leon picks it up, I have less than a second to decide to sprint after him. If I wait a second, or jog for the first couple of yards, I don't make that play."

The message, Beebe hopes when he speaks to groups, transcends athletics.

"It doesn't have to be sports," he said. "If it's a life or death thing, and a kid has only a second to react, hopefully he or she will make the right decision. I reacted in the right way because that's how my parents brought me up. If you beat your children and neglect them, and tell them they're no good, you've decreased that kid's chance of making it in this world."

Beebe has prayed for Lett, who is still with Dallas but didn't play in the first part of the 1997 season because of a drug suspension.

"I like Leon. Not only is he one of the best defensive linemen in the league, he's a nice person," Beebe said. "When *Sports Illustrated* called to get me and Leon together for a follow up story, because people were still talking about the play months later, I said yes, I'd do it. I was vacationing in West Palm Beach, ironically, with Frank Reich, and our wives."

"When I first saw Leon drive up in his car, I went up and told him I agreed to do it on only one condition," Beebe said. "Leon said, 'What condition?' I said, 'That there's no physical abuse.' He laughed. Leon is a good guy. A very reserved, shy gentleman, doesn't say a whole lot, just a good guy. To tell you the truth, I felt bad for him."

The following season during a Thanksgiving Day game in Miami, Lett again made national headlines for a mistake.

After a missed field goal by Miami, all Dallas had to do was let the ball stop rolling, and it would take over. On the slippery turf, Lett followed the ball as if it were his own child. However, he touched the ball, Miami recovered and went on to win.

"That put even more pressure on him. I prayed for him, that the media would let up on him," Beebe said. "The hate mail and the racial mail from the Super Bowl was just so horrible. He was getting death threats. You never know when some whacko is going to try to whack you. It's a crying shame we live in a world like that. It's just wrong. The money bet on these games, that's where that stuff starts from, where the hate mail for Leon came in. I felt for him. I'm not saying the drug suspensions were the direct results of this, but the additional pressures on this private, shy guy had to be overwhelming on him and his family."

Reggie White, an All-Pro defensive end for Green Bay and Beebe's teammate in 1996 during the Packers' Super Bowl season, said Beebe opened his eyes that day.

"Of all the people you'd think would make a play like that, you'd have to think of Don first," White said. "Of course, I thought about it. And when I pick up a fumble, I'm keeping the ball high from now on. I owe than one to Don."

The play was all about a message that Beebe believes had nothing to do with showboating, and everything to do with God.

"The Lord used that play to make me recognizable, so people could read my story and know what I'm about," Beebe said. "I realize that I'm not in football for the fame and fortune and everything that goes with it. Those are gifts from God. I look at it, and this is what the Lord had planned for me. The reason I'm in it is to touch people's lives, for Jesus Christ. I'm not going to take personal things, money or anything to heaven, but I am going to take you. Whoever you are, who I've come into contact with, is going to heaven. This is such a short, minute period of time on eternity's scale, that you can't even measure it probably. But people have a hard time seeing the big picture."

E.J. Montini, a columnist for the *Arizona Republic*, felt Beebe was the star of the game. Here's Montini's column from the *Republic:*

> *It was the most important judgment call made during last weekend's Super Bowl, and they blew it. The sportswriters and commentators covering the game picked Dallas Cowboys quarterback Troy Aikman as the "Most Valuable Player."*
>
> *There should have been an instant-replay official working inside the press box. Without a doubt, this call should be overturned.*
>
> *I can see how the writers might have named Aikman "Most Talented Player" or "Most Effective Player," or even "Most Stereotypically Good-Looking Player," but it was simply, factually incorrect to select Aikman as the "Most Valuable Player."*
>
> *The most valuable player of Super Bowl XXVII, hands down, was Buffalo Bills wide receiver Don Beebe.*
>
> *No one else was even close.*

Still, Aikman walked off with the MVP award, primarily because those making the decision allowed themselves to be swayed by insignificant details like statistics and, even worse, results.

Aikman threw four touchdown passes. He gave up no interceptions. He did not fumble the ball. In fact, he recovered a fumble. He also ran like a deer. And, as you know, his team won.

All of which qualified Aikman to become the "Most Financially Rewarded Player," the "Most Interviewed Player" and the "Most Likely to Make An I'm Going to Disneyland Commercial," which he did. But Aikman just wasn't the most valuable player.

For that honor, there simply was no choice but Beebe.

The receiver for the Bills did not have a perfect game, like Aikman. He dropped a pass in the end zone. He managed to catch two other passes, including one for a 40-yard touchdown, and that didn't happen until the third quarter, and by then, the game was over. Everybody, including Beebe, knew it. Still, there's no doubt Beebe was the most valuable player.

The evidence is a single play.

It was late in the fourth quarter, only five minutes left, and the Bills were losing, 52-17. Everyone was eager for the game to be over. The Cowboys were on their bench, waving towels. The Bills were sitting on their bench, covering their heads with towels.

With the ball near the Cowboys 35-yard line, Bills quarterback Frank Reich went back to pass. Beebe ran downfield on a pattern. The Cowboys' rush swarmed over Reich, forcing a fumble. A huge defensive tackle named Leon Lett picked up the ball and headed downfield for what looked like a certain touchdown.

Later, recalling what happened, one of the Cowboys said, "That guy who caught up to (Lett) ran past us like we were standing still."

It was Beebe.

When Lett reached the 5-yard line, he held out his arms, the ball in one hand, and began taking long, exaggerated steps. It was part celebration, part boustful showmanship. Just before Lett got to the goal line, however, Beebe, who had been chasing Lett down the field, caught up to him, slapping the ball from Lett's hand. The two of them stumbled over the goal line as the ball rolled through the end zone for a touchback.

Dallas got no touchdown, no points.

After the game, reporters gathered around Lett, who jokingly told them he'd learned a lesson about not acting like a hot dog until after you cross the goal line. In all the hundreds of stories written about the game, though, I found only a few that quoted Beebe. He said, "I was brought up never to quit, and I don't care what the score is."

Beebe could have given up the chase. Everyone else on his side had quit by then. The coaches, the other players, the fans. But not him. He ran Lett down. Even now, it's the one play from the game I can replay in my mind, the sight of the small receiver flashing up behind the hulking lineman.

Aikman, without a doubt, earned his team a victory. He earned millions of dollars for himself in future endorsements, and millions more for the Dallas franchise. His performance certainly did generate profit.

Don Beebe, on the other hand, gave us something of real value.

Bill Polian (left) and John Butler. Both were general managers for the Buffalo Bills and two of Don's favorite people in football. "Thanks for all the memories. You two are the best.

Don and his good friend Bill Brooks, celebrating a touchdown in 1993.

Don and his good friend Scott Berchtold who works in the
Public Relations Dept. of the Buffalo Bills. Scott is holding
a 5-lb. smallmouth bass caught on Lake Erie. "Oh, by the
way, mine was 6 pounds."

15

THE GREATEST COMEBACK IN NFL HISTORY

One of the best playoff memories—one of the Bills' greatest wins ever—came on January 3, 1993, against Houston in the AFC Wildcard playoff game.

The game didn't start out that way. The Bills were getting thumped, 28-3, casting a somber cloud over the Bills' locker room at halftime. Beebe and pal Steve Tasker, a wide receiver and special teams All-Pro for the Bills, chatted.

"We're sitting in the locker room, me and Tasker, talking about where we'd be playing golf next week," Beebe said. "We never gave up, but it still looked like the season was over."

"We got together before we went out for the second half

and said, 'Hey, look let's start making plays.' We weren't going to give up, even if we ended up getting beat, 50-3."

It looked like 50-3 might be a good guess when the second half started.

"First series, second play, Houston's Bubba McDowell intercepts it and goes for a touchdown," Beebe said. "We're down, 35-3, and walking off the field, 'It's over.' The only person who was positive on the sideline was Frank Reich. He was going up and down the bench, saying, 'This game is not over guys. Let's just starting making plays.' Sure enough, plays start coming by the bunches."

Reich said he was moved to act that day, unaware of what was in store.

"I wasn't, to tell you the truth, thinking we would come back, or that we would not come back," Reich said. "We were just talking about what we needed to do, to make a few first downs, score a few points and make it respectable. Just more of a play-by-play, touchdown-by-touchdown scenario. It's just kind of like life, when you are overwhelmed with circumstances that seem impossible to get out. It's no different in football. You just put your faith in it, and move forward."

Reich hit Beebe with a 38-yard touchdown pass, starting a streak of four straight touchdown passes that Reich and the Bills used to pull off a stunning comeback.

"Frank said in the huddle that I should be aware, that he might come to me," Beebe said. "He said that a lot, to be aware, because he's a really smart quarterback. On the touchdown play, the ball was supposed to go to (tight end) Pete Metzelaars. But it was a blown coverage. I got pushed wide, wide enough where I stepped on the (out of bounds) line. Frank hit me, and I just walked into the end zone."

"I was fortunate to score one of the touchdowns to get the ball rolling," Beebe said. "Frank hit Andre Reed with a couple more, and we end up winning in overtime, 41-38."

The memory is fond, Reich said, in no small part because of Beebe's involvement.

"That's definitely the big thrill of it—that you're doing something like this with your best friend," Reich said. "Sharing that moment is what makes football such a great sport, good memories like that through the years. Throwing that first touchdown pass to Don—there's no one I'd rather have it go to."

"It was the greatest comeback in NFL history," Beebe said. "It might be the greatest game in NFL history. It's a great story of what happened, to hear Frank tell it. The night before the game, Frank was listening to the song, *In Christ Alone* by Michael English. It's a great song, and it tells a great story. This song touched Frank's life."

In Christ Alone
Co-written by Shawn Craig and Don Koch

In Christ alone will I glory, though I could pride myself in battles won

For I've been blessed beyond measure and by His strength alone I overcome

Oh, I could stop and count successes like diamonds in my hand

But those trophies could not equal to the grace by which I stand

(Chorus):
In Christ alone I place my trust, And find my glory in the power of the cross
In every victory let it be said of me, my source of strength, my source of hope is Christ alone

In Christ alone will I glory for only by his grace I am redeemed
And only his tender mercy could reach beyond my weakness to my need
Now, I seek no greater honor than just to know Him more
And to count my gains but losses, And to the glory of my Lord

"The morning of the game," Beebe said, "Frank said he listened to that song over and over. He knew God was going to use that song, that day, for some reason. He didn't know what it would entail. He was just going to let God work.

"Well, after the game was over, the greatest comeback in NFL history, Frank went down to the podium in the interview room. He asked everyone to wait. He went up and got the words to the song, wrote them down, and read it to the national media. Millions were watching. It was so moving, just incredible."

Don tries to elude a would-be tackler in a game against the Indianapolis Colts.

16

DEALING WITH
SUPER BOWL DEFEATS

Super Bowl XXV: Beebe was injured and missed perhaps the most exciting Super Bowl in the 1990s. A missed field goal by the Bills at the end of the game cost them a 20-19 defeat at the hands of the New York Giants.

Super Bowl XXVI: "We played a good game against Washington. But we had six turnovers. I ended up with a touchdown catch. *Sports Illustrated* had a picture of it, Darrell Green in the picture, and that's good, because Green is one of the best cornerbacks ever to play the game. But it didn't mean anything because my team was getting beaten and the game was over at that point. I just threw the ball down after the touchdown because, to me, it meant nothing. I'm glad the equipment guy ran and got the ball for me. Because down the road, it'll mean something. It does a little now, that I scored in the Super Bowl. Down the road for my kids, it'll mean more."

Washington pounded the Bills, 37-24.

That season was a breakout year in another way, as Beebe set a Bills' regular season record with four touchdown catches in one game against Pittsburgh. In that game, Beebe caught 10 passes for 112 yards.

Super Bowl XXVII: The Bills fell apart and lost 52-17, but Beebe was America's choice for Most Valuable Player for the play on Leon Lett.

"Every time we had a breakdown," Beebe said, "it resulted in six for Dallas."

Super Bowl XXVIII: Another blowout loss, again to Dallas, this one a 30-13 affair.

Beebe had a strong game, pulling in six catches for 60 yards. Beebe also returned a kickoff for 34 yards, the longest kickoff return in Bills' Super Bowl history.

"In Super Bowl XXVIII, this is the biggest example of not handling adversity, because we were beating down Dallas in that first half," Beebe said. "There's no question in my mind that we should have won that game. We had another turnover in the second half and we couldn't overcome it."

Beebe's performance that day drew plenty of praise.

"I wish we all had been as focused as Don was for the Super Bowl," Buffalo quarterback Jim Kelly told reporters after the game. "Probably a lot didn't notice, but Don Beebe had a good game. I think it was a game that may put him over the hump as a player. It should give him a lot of confidence for the future."

The losses in the Super Bowls were hard to deal with in one way because the Bills wore a label of loser in the media despite being the AFC Champions four years in a row.

"From a football perspective," Reich said, "even though there was so much negative press to losing a Super Bowl, or in our case, multiple Super Bowls, just to get there four times was incredible. It's not your goal to get there and lose. But to get there—you have to take some satisfaction from that. By no means are you satisfied coming in second. But still, we were the only ones from the AFC there."

Beebe said there was an unexplainable difference between the Buffalo teams that lost the Super Bowls and the Green Bay team that won in 1997.

"I have been asked this question: 'What's the difference between Green Bay and the Bills teams?'" Beebe said. "Offensively, they are very similar. Two Hall of Fame quarterbacks, great wide receivers, great running backs, and great offensive lines. Defensively, I believe Green Bay is a little better.

"The biggest difference that I can tell you would be the way the teams faced adversity during the Super Bowl. In every game at some point in time, you face adversity, meaning you have a turnover, a blown play, a crucial penalty—something that goes wrong that could have a negative effect on the outcome of the game. It's how a team faces those situations that often makes the difference between winning and losing.

"Football is such an emotional game, and when you play in the Super Bowl, emotions are much greater. At

Buffalo, during the course of the season in big games when we faced adversity, we handled it very well. But in the Super Bowl we didn't. For example, Super Bowl XXVI, we gave the Washington Redskins six turnovers. In Super Bowl XXVII, we gave the Cowboys nine turnovers. And in Super Bowl XXVIII, we gave Dallas three crucial turnovers in the second half. My best example would be Super Bowl XXVIII when we were beating Dallas in the first half and we came out in the second half and had a fumble that they recovered and scored on. It was like a needle in a balloon from that point on. Emotionally, we just didn't handle that adversity.

"On the other hand, Green Bay faced very similar adversity in the fact that we went up 10-0 in the first quarter and found ourselves down quickly, 14-10. But the Packers had the right frame of mind, meaning we weren't about to let the New England Patriots take the game away from us. We went out there in the second quarter, kept our frame of mind, and ended up ahead, 27-14, at the half. The result was an easy victory in Super Bowl XXXI.

"That is the biggest difference between the two teams." Beebe said. "Why that is, I don't know. It just is."

Don and friends. Jim Kelly (12), Andre Reed, and Kent Hull celebrate a Beebe touchdown in Buffalo.

17

BLIP ON THE GRIDIRON RESUME

If Beebe had his way, he would have stayed in Buffalo for the 1995 season—and any seasons thereafter, for that matter. But Buffalo chose not to re-sign Beebe.

However, he was rewarded by Carolina with a two-year, $1.3 million contract. Plus, Frank Reich and Pete Metzelaars were also headed to Carolina.

"I wanted to stay in Buffalo my whole career," Beebe said. "John Butler (the general manager, since former GM Bill Polian went to Carolina) liked me, but they wanted to go a different direction. They had some young guys."

Before Beebe considered Carolina, he asked his agent to inquire about Green Bay.

"I wanted to play for Green Bay, because I thought they

were close to winning the Super Bowl," Beebe said. "But I went to Carolina when that didn't work out."

Speaking of not working out...

"It was like a storybook thing to go to Carolina together," Reich said. "I mean, me and my favorite receiver, my best friend. We got to go start with an expansion franchise. It seemed too good to be true."

What's that saying? If it seems too good to be true, then it's...

"Carolina was tough," Beebe said. "That was the hardest year, at least for football. The third week of camp, I had been starting and I broke a rib. I never did get the starting job back. I really had high expectations being the starting guy for a team in its first season. Going in there, being the No. 1 guy... I had never had that before. But without Andre Reed, that was the big thing, I was going to do it. (The Carolina assistant coaches) made me feel like the previous six years I played with Buffalo weren't there, that I couldn't perform at that level. It got worse and worse as the season went on."

Reich didn't have much fun either.

"Don got hurt and didn't get to play much," Reich said. "I got benched three games into it. It had to be one of the toughest years, football-wise. It was so strange, you just knew God was in control. I know whatever it is, God will be in control. But at first, especially, it didn't make sense."

Polian, Carolina's first and only general manager, said Beebe, Reich, and Metzelaars did contribute to the growth of the young organization.

"We started out 0-5 that first year," Polian said. "Without the work ethic of Don, Pete, and Frank, and their professionalism, I don't know that we'd have gotten out of that hole, or what it would've done to the franchise to not have players with that kind of character around. We were able to rebound from that tough time because of them. In turn, that allowed us to experience success soon afterward."

Polian, who helped build Carolina into a power quickly —the Panthers played in the NFC Championship in only their second year (and ended up losing to Beebe and the Packers), has nothing but fond memories of Beebe.

"Certainly, I hope Don has no bad blood because there's none on my part," Polian said. "He got hurt early, and never was able to really get back—he never really had a chance here to show what he could do."

Looking back, Beebe understands.

"I firmly believe that the Carolina situation was not football," Beebe said. "God wanted me there for other reasons. I learned from that. It was a tough year. But it was a good part of my Christian walk."

Beebe dealt with more media criticism than ever before, questioning his attitude and toughness.

"It made me think, 'Just whose opinion am I concerned about here, the assistant coaches, the media or God's opinion of me?'" Beebe said. "I came to the realization that God is right, that I won't listen to what some others are saying. 'I'm just going to listen to You, God, and whatever He has to say is what I'm going to adhere to and what I'm going to do.'"

Along the way, Frank, Pete, and Don did business with the same realtor, Linda Davis.

"We met two of our best friends, Buck and Linda Davis," Beebe said. "Had we not gone to Charlotte, we wouldn't have ever met them. Linda accepted Jesus Christ as her personal savior, and Buck rededicated his Christianity, and we felt it was a gift from God to be a part of it. So obviously, it wasn't just football—Buck and Linda were two of many reasons why we were sent there. It took a while for me to learn that."

"A while" meant the whole season in Carolina.

"To start for a team that went to four Super Bowls and play every down and then come to Carolina to an expansion team, and not play a lot, or being a big part of it, was strange," Beebe said. "Two reasons I came were Bill Polian, one of my favorite people in football, and Frank Reich. Pete Metzelaars was there too, and he's a good friend. But as I said, going to Charlotte was not about football. The Lord had different plans. Through my Christian walk, I matured a lot. I came to rely more on God than on the media's criticism. That was the biggest thing I learned there."

Beebe, close to Nicolau and then receivers coach Charlie Joiner, who succeeded Nicolau in Buffalo, never hit it off with the assistants in Carolina. But Beebe does hold Panthers' coach Dom Capers in the highest regard.

"The offensive coordinator and receiver coach made it tough for me to enjoy," Beebe said. "I love Dom Capers. I think Dom is an A-plus coach, a real gentlemen. Bill Polian, I like him, too, he's top notch. And Carolina as a whole is a great, great organization."

Beebe started only once and caught 14 passes, including

three games in which he caught three passes each. He returned to Chadron in the spring of 1996 to complete his degree in marketing and management. In addition to organizing his annual benefit golf tourney for Chadron State, which he's done since 1989, Beebe earned a 4.0 and made the President's List. He also got a phone call from Dom Capers in February. Actually, Diana answered the phone.

"We knew the call was coming," Diana said. "I told Dom how much we enjoyed living in Charlotte, and how much the opportunity meant to Don and I. He, of course, didn't tell me he was going to release Don, he just said he needed to talk to Don. And Dom was so nice, such a good person. I told him Don would be back early in the afternoon."

Early in the afternoon, Capers called again.

"It was a relief when Dom called," Beebe said. "At that time, I didn't know Frank (to the Jets and then Lions) would be gone, and Pete, too (to Detroit). On the phone, Dom was a true gentleman. I couldn't have had more respect for him and the way he handled the situation."

"Don," Capers said, "we're going to go ahead and release you."

Although Beebe knew it was coming, it was a strange feeling.

"I had never faced that before," Beebe said. "I faced it with a good attitude. I said, 'Dom, you're a heckuva coach and a good person. It was a special thing to be a part of the inaugural season of the organization.' He went on to say a lot of nice things about me. He said, 'I thought you were a great receiver, it just didn't work out.' I wasn't the taller, physical guy that the offensive coordinator and receivers coach wanted. Dom could've handled that in a less compassionate, callous way. But Dom Capers is a classy man and Carolina is a great organization."

Playing for Capers, despite the fallout from the whole season, was still positive.

"I've been fortunate, because I have played for three great coaches in Marv (Levy), Dom, and Mike Holmgren," Beebe said. "I continued to grow as a Christian. If I hadn't gone there, I wouldn't have grown. People kept writing, 'What's wrong with Beebe?' I finally got to the point of, 'Who do I listen to? It came down to who am I relying on?' And that answer is, the Lord."

Had one of Beebe's former coaches had it his way, Beebe would have never ended up in Carolina, but would have been with an expansion team nonetheless.

"When Don left (Buffalo) and became available," said former Bills receivers coach Nick Nicolau, "I had already left and was at Jacksonville. I made a strong case to get him. But (the Jaguar coaches and management) felt Don was on in years. They meant chronological age, because he was already past 30. But because of the time away from college when he was hanging siding, he hadn't played that many years in the NFL."

Carolina? Just the short stay. Jacksonville? It wasn't in the plan. But what was?

The greatest couple you'all could ever want to meet: dear friends from Charlotte, Buck and Linda Davis.

Don gave the invocation at his graduation from Chardon State College in 1996.

Preparing for another victory at Lambeau Field. Brett Favre is quite a prankster. Left to right: Brett Favre, Don, Desmond Howard, Antonio Freeman, and Robert Brooks.

18

WARMING A CAREER ON THE FROZEN TUNDRA

After the Bills decided not to re-sign Beebe after the 1994 season, he really wanted to go to Green Bay. When that didn't work, he went to Carolina for one season. When that did not work, he looked toward Green Bay again. It got to the point where he'd go to Green Bay—or nowhere.

That's right, Beebe was ready to become a full-time father. Even after he signed with Green Bay, he worried that the fire inside had dimmed. He also knew how much he did not like being away from his wife and children.

"I was thinking about retiring," Beebe said. "Last year (before the 1996 season), I contemplated retiring. I was at the point where my kids were getting older. I wanted to be with them. I didn't want to go to training camp and be away from them for six weeks."

Beebe sought answers where he always has.

"I was praying, 'Lord, I kind of want to retire. If You want me in football, I will still do Your will. But I asked God to give me a rejuvenated spirit to go out there and enjoy what I'm doing and give it the effort I've always done. I can't do it half-hearted,'" Beebe said. "The next day I went to practice, and I had a rejuvenated spirit. I was full of spirit, and I enjoyed being out there. From that point on, I've enjoyed being here every day."

Folks wondered whether there was room for Beebe on a team so talented and deep with wide receivers, especially with the addition of Desmond Howard and the maturing of Antonio Freeman as a complement to Robert Brooks.

"Even though people were doubting me, I knew I'd make the team," Beebe said. "I knew the Lord was using me to speak to the people in Green Bay, Wisconsin."

But basically as a stranger, someone who had played in the AFC, except for the year in Carolina, Packer fans knew little of Beebe—except, of course, the play on Leon Lett in the Super Bowl.

"I knew I was going to do something during the season," Beebe said. "I didn't know what. Because people don't listen to someone who doesn't do something. People listen to winners, not losers—it's sad to say. They're more likely to listen to a Reggie White than a backup, or a star quarterback instead of a practice squad quarterback just because that's how people are."

Beebe opened October with a bang, returning a kickoff

90 yards for a touchdown against one of Green Bay's biggest rivals, Chicago. The next game, injuries threw Beebe into the starting lineup, and he had the biggest game of his career during a Monday night win over San Francisco, catching 11 passes for 220 yards.

"The kickoff return against Chicago and then came the Monday night game—the big plays really helped me build a relationship with the people in Green Bay," Beebe said. "I really grew to like the people in Green Bay. Wherever I've gone the feedback has been great. The people in Green Bay are blue-collar people, like the people in Buffalo, they appreciate guys who work hard. They like guys who sacrifice for the team, not 'me' guys."

Beebe made it clear that he wasn't a "me" guy when he showed up at training camp at St. Norbert College.

"One of the first things I said in camp when I was asked what my goals were—I said, 'All I want is to go to the Super Bowl and win, I want to know what that feels like. If it's carrying water to Reggie White when he's tired, I'll do that,'" Beebe said. "People read that and thought it was funny, but it was true—I'd do it. People in Green Bay like the team goals. In that aspect, people liked me, and I liked them. It was a neat relationship. I don't care what my role is, first receiver, second receiver, third receiver, fourth receiver, kick returner—I was fortunate to be all of those last year. I think people like the small guy who shouldn't have made it. The guy who was told he was too small, went to too small of a college. People just like the underdog —everyone always wants to root for the underdog. And I've always been the underdog."

His agent, Bob LaMonte, agrees.

"Don Beebe," LaMonte said, "is the little choo-choo train that could. That's a lot of the mystique about Don, about how he's defied all the odds. He's small for an NFL player, yet 1997 is his ninth year in the NFL. The broken leg, and how he came back. He just keeps coming back."

Had the big games that came at crucial times not come, Beebe wonders what his role would have been as far as his faith is concerned.

"If I didn't have the kind of year I had last year, I wouldn't have gotten that kind of response and been able to share my faith, even though we won the Super Bowl," Beebe said.

The Packers were also appealing because of their image: A team owned by the public in a not-so-major market that had a tradition second to none and insisted on signing players with good character.

"They had Reggie White and a few other mature Christians," Beebe said. "They signed Eugene Robinson, a devout Christian. Keith Jackson was there too, so I knew it was a mature group and that God would use that in a positive way. It was neat to see how last year turned out. The world really looked among the Green Bay Packers as a good Christian, worldly-valued team. That's kind of neat to be a part of that."

One of Beebe's good friends on the team is Brett Favre. The two play a lot of golf together.

"It drives Don crazy because he always tells you, 'Good shot' when you hit a good one or just compliments something," Favre said. "But I'm not like that, I'm not going to give someone I'm trying to beat a compliment."

"I call him a front-running Jessie," Beebe said with a laugh. "He's beating you on the course or hitting good shots, and he's all talkative and nice. But he has a bad hole, and he gets quiet, won't say a word."

Beebe's face gets serious when asked about Favre's situation before the Super Bowl season, where Favre admitted an addiction to a painkiller and sought treatment. "Brett is awesome, not just as a quarterback, but as a person," Beebe said. "The whole Vicodin deal—a lot of people wouldn't have said a word. But Brett stepped forward and said, 'I have a problem here, I'd like to get it solved.' It made it easier for him to solve it after getting it out in the open. I respect him so much for that. He's not perfect. I'm not perfect. Nobody else is perfect."

Another close friend is Reggie White, who helped Beebe at a football camp Beebe put on after the Super Bowl when one of Beebe's close friends died. Beebe wanted to raise money for his friend's widow and two young children. White volunteered to go right away, and asked only for two big pieces of cake from Beebe's mother, Barb, in the family kitchen in Sugar Grove, Illinois.

"Before I came here, I heard a lot about Reggie White, how he is the greatest Christian ever to play sports, the best lineman and so on," Beebe said. "Reggie is everything you hear about him, and he's more. It's all legit, the man's for real. He's a man of God, and he has his perspective right. He has compassion like nobody I've ever seen. He's a good friend and always will be. We hit it off really well."

On the field and off, the Packers were a hit.

19
GREEN BAY, 1996:
THE FIRST STEPS
IN THE
RETURN TO GLORY

ackers 34, Buccaneers 3 (Sept. 1): The Packers rolled up 24 first-half points as quarterback Brett Favre hit Keith Jackson for three touchdown passes in the first two quarters. Chris Jacke added field goals of 23 and 40 yards for Green Bay. Favre finished the scoring with a one-yard toss to Dorsey Levens in the third quarter. The game was a statistical nightmare for Tampa Bay, which gained only 176 yards of total offense, compared to Green Bay's 406. Favre got off to a solid start, completing 20-of-27 passes for 247 yards and no interceptions.

"I felt going down to Tampa, winning on the road in the first game of the season, was a step in the right direction," Beebe said. "But I knew in training camp that this team was something special. But to come out and beat them that bad, it was obvious we had a lot of talent."

The Packers outrushed the Bucs more than two-to-one, with Green Bay picking up 139 yards, led by Edgar Bennett's 62 yards on 13 carries, compared to only 59 for Tampa Bay.

Packers 39, Philadelphia 13 (Sept. 9): The Packers played their first home game of the season against the Eagles in their first home appearance on Monday Night Football in a decade capitalizing on four first half Eagles' turnovers and totaling 432 yards, the Packers easily ran their record to 2-0.

"For us, that was a big game on national television on a Monday night," Beebe said. "To beat a team as good as Philadelphia, as handily as we did, put a benchmark out for the rest of the season that the Packers are for real."

Doug Evans intercepted a Rodney Peete pass at the 14-yard line right off the bat, which set up a 29-yard field goal. Two exchanges later, Sean Jones forced a Ricky Watters fumble that was recovered by Brian Williams. Brett Favre, who did not complete a pass in his first five throws, hit Robert Brooks with a 25-yard touchdown pass to put Green Bay up, 10-0. The Packers weren't done as they put 20 unanswered points on the board in the second quarter, with Favre directing scoring drives of 77, 52, and 75 yards. Green Bay had a 30-7 lead at halftime and then never looked back in the second half.

Packers 42, Chargers 10 (Sept. 15): For the first time in 14 years, the Packers opened the season 3-0. Their third straight win of the season came at the expense of San Diego. Green Bay dominated all aspects of the game. The Pack had 349 yards to only 141 for San Diego, outrushed the Chargers 132 to 33, passed for 217 while holding the Chargers to 108, and held the ball for 11 minutes longer than the Chargers.

"Coach Holmgren talked about going 3-0 early in the season," Beebe said. "Because to get out of the box early and go 3-0, it would be big. We ended up winning against a very good San Diego team, and beating them pretty good."

Green Bay held the Chargers without a first down following the opening kickoff and marched down the field 55 yards in six plays for take a 7-0 lead. After a San Diego field goal to close the gap to 7-3, the Chargers would get no closer. In the second quarter, Green Bay had drives of 80 yards on six plays; 88 yards, capped by a 19-yard touchdown pass from Favre to Antonio Freeman, and posted another six points on a 17-play, 88-yard drive that ended with an eight-yard TD strike to William Henderson, putting Green Bay up, 21-3, at halftime. The Packers blew the game open in the third quarter when Favre hit tight end Keith Jackson with a seven-yard touchdown. San Diego's only touchdown of the game came with eight minutes left in the final quarter, and was just the second touchdown allowed by the Packer defense through the opening three games of the season.

Packers running back Edgar Bennett lost a fumble, which drew attention because it was only his first after 726 flawless carries. LeRoy Butler, the inventor of the Lambeau Leap into the stands, got to hone his craft when he intercepted a pass and returned it 90 yards for a touchdown to push Green Bay's lead to 25, 35-10. Desmond Howard gave a preview of things to come when he returned a punt 65 yards for the Pack's final touchdown, with just under five minutes remaining in the game.

Vikings 30, Packers 21 (Sept. 22): The Packers took their first lost of the season. Host Minnesota trailed, 21-17, in the third quarter. But the Vikings got a 37-yard touchdown run by Robert Smith and two field goals to complete a 13-0 fourth quarter to take the win.

One bright spot was Beebe, who had three catches for 96 yards, including an 80-yard touchdown catch from Favre in the third quarter.

"It seems like the last few years Green Bay has always had trouble at Minnesota," Beebe said. "Like a bad golf hole, one that you just can't par no matter what, Minnesota is just a place where we don't play well. And it happened again this time. We had the game, could've won it. After we scored that long touchdown, we got an interception by George Koonce who returned it for another touchdown. I thought we had the game won at that point. But they took it in and scored. It was a tough loss."

Packers 31, Seahawks 10 (Sept. 29): Host Seattle wasn't much of a challenge as the Packers opened up a 17-0 lead in the second quarter and never let Seattle back in it. Bennett had a big day rushing the ball, with 22 carries for 94 yards as Green Bay had 344 yards of total offense, including 142 on the ground. Seattle was close in total yards, with 329, but the quality of numbers paled from there. Seattle completed only 11 of 34 passes and was intercepted four times. Favre was nearly perfect, with no interceptions while hitting Antonio Freeman twice for TDs and completing 20 of 34 passes for 209 yards. Beebe had two catches for 15 yards.

"It's always tough to win in Seattle, in that dome," Beebe said. "It doesn't matter how good or bad that team is. To tell you the truth, we had more fans than they did. In Minnesota, Tampa, and Seattle, we had more fans than they did. It was louder for our opening lineup than for theirs. On a national level, the Green Bay Packers are big."

Packers 37, Bears 6 (Oct. 6): Beebe returned a kickoff 90 yards after a field goal to spark a route of his hometown team, the Chicago Bears.

"That play, I felt like the second-fastest I ever felt—and the fastest I ever felt on a football field," Beebe said. "At Chadron State, I ran a 4.21 for the Jets before the draft, and that was the fastest I have ever felt. But against Chicago, it was something. It was perfect timing—I had never returned a kickoff, and it happened to go for a touchdown at the field I lived near growing up, against the team I had rooted for. It was one of the greatest moments of my career."

Green Bay finished its first of two three-game road trips at Soldier Field. It left the Packers tied for first with the

Vikings in the NFC Central.

"It's always big to win on the road," Beebe said. "When you can win at Soldier Field, it's a big win. You have to win them all at home and win at least half on the road. If you do that, you go at least 12-4. You do that, you probably get home field advantage."

Favre continued his record-pace of touchdown tosses, hitting four for the third time in the six games, giving him 20 touchdown passes for the young season. Favre's third touchdown of the game came as time expired in the first half when he hit Freeman with a 50-yard "Hail Mary" pass. It was one of two touchdowns for Freeman, who finished the game with a career-high 146 yards on seven catches.

All areas of the team contributed to the win. Despite the offense getting blanked in the first quarter, it scored 20 points in the second and added 14 in the third to ice the game. The Bears offense was stymied by the Packers' defense, finishing with 243 yards. Additionally, the Pack intercepted three Dave Krieg passes.

Favre finished the game with 18 completions out of 27 attempts, with one interception, just his third of the season.

The Packers were off to a Super Bowl start at 5-1, but the best was yet to come.

Don celebrates a great win over the San Francisco 49ers on ABC Monday Night Football in 1996 with Coach Mike Holmgren (center) and Don's agent Bob LaMonte.

Don has said many times that Melissa Stanton's courage in her battle against cancer has been an inspiration to him. That inspiration came in handy against the 49ers.

20
A MONDAY NIGHT
TO REMEMBER

$\mathbf{J}$t's called a "defining moment."

Not all players have one. Many languish on the sidelines—should they ever get a shot in the first place. Not all answer the bell, not all ever recover from NOT being able to rise to the occasion. Special situations call for special people.

Backs are pushed to the wall. Who will swing back? Who will step forward? Who will sacrifice when the time comes, and then leave it all out on the field?

On Monday night, October 14, 1996, the Packers needed a win over San Francisco. The Packers were 5-1, but only one of those wins came against a team that would end up with a winning season. So much tangible—and intangible

—was on the line. In practical terms, the two teams were trying to get an early leg up on probably not just the Playoffs, but home field advantage. Intangibly, the game, to many, could be a signal of a gridiron sort of changing of the guard, with long-time power San Francisco and its aging cast of veterans getting pushed out of the picture by the younger, up-and-coming Packers.

However, if the Pack was going to be back and announce its arrival on the most watched game of the NFL each week—ABC's Monday Night Football—it was going to have to do it without leading receiver Robert Brooks, although Green Bay didn't know it, because Brooks would be injured on the first offensive play of the game.

So, are you ready for some football?

Don Beebe was.

San Francisco took a 17-6 lead at halftime, an 11-point margin for a team that knows a thing or two about how to win a big game. But that wasn't enough. Because Beebe turned in the game of his life, catching 11 passes for 220 yards, including a 59-yard touchdown strike from quarterback Brett Favre. The touchdown catch gave Beebe his first chance to attempt the "Lambeau Leap," in which players, upon scoring, jump into the stands in the end zone.

"That's not the kind of thing I'd do usually, but I'd have been run out of town if I broke with that tradition," Beebe said with a smile. "But I did it, and it was incredible. I was worried the fans wouldn't let me back out. I like it now because it gets the fans involved."

Beebe caught everything thrown his way, and then some. In overtime, the Packers came out on top, 23-20.

"I've never felt so fast," Beebe said. "The week before against Chicago on that 90-yard kickoff (return for a touchdown), I felt like I was flying, too."

Beebe knew he had played a solid role in the win, but didn't know how big until ABC sideline reporter Lynn Swann caught up to him after the game for an interview.

"Do you know how many catches you had, and yards," Swann yelled as the full house at Lambeau Field cheered Beebe.

"No," Don said. "What, 130, maybe 140 yards?"

"Try eleven catches and 220 yards!" Swann told Beebe.

Coach Mike Holmgren, a key figure in acquiring Beebe, knew someone had to step up.

"The little guy can play, can't he?" Holmgren said. "What a great effort tonight, and we needed it. We lose Robert on the first play. Desmond Howard was a big factor tonight as well, but Don Beebe came through big, big tonight."

A friend from his Buffalo days was cheering as loud as anyone.

"I sat down and wrote Don a letter after that game," said Bill Polian, Carolina's general manager. "I was so proud of him. But that night didn't surprise me because he's still one of the fastest guys in the league and he can catch. Don seems to always play a major role in big games."

Beebe could not stop thinking about Brooks after the game.

"For me, eleven catches is big, and it was fun—(but) there's a good part and bad part of this," Beebe said. "I really feel bad for Robert. He is such a huge part of this team. Having him gone for the year makes me sad. I wish he could be a part of this."

Antonio Freeman knew that given the chance, Beebe would respond.

"That's what he's being doing for eight years in this league," Freeman said. "He's just a competitor who makes the sacrifice for the team and then is always there when you need him."

Previously, Beebe's big game had come his third year in Buffalo in a game against Pittsburgh in which Beebe caught four touchdown passes, tying a team record.

"The four touchdown catches against Pittsburgh were big, but we kind of blew that team out," Beebe said. "The way this game turned out—going into overtime—this is probably my biggest game in helping a team out. Getting some big yardage in key situations feels good."

Holmgren, a former coordinator for the 49ers, knew the road to the top of the mountain for Green Bay had to go through the 49ers at some point.

"This is a great win for the team, for the fans," Holmgren said. "Monday Night Football in Green Bay— maybe now we will have a couple more next year, I hope. It was just one of those great games."

Beebe, a veteran of four AFC Championships with the Bills, also knows the big kid on the block rules until someone proves otherwise.

"In order to be the best, you have to beat the best," Beebe said. "We had to beat this team if we wanted to be on top of the league. The 49ers will be there in the Playoffs. We'll probably face them again. They're a great team.

We're playing well right now. This was a huge win for us."

Favre, one of Beebe's biggest supporters from the first day of Beebe's first minicamp earlier in the spring, was overjoyed for Beebe—although Favre was a bit exhausted after throwing 61 passes.

"Don Beebe did it today," Favre said. "It was unbelievable."

It was also unbelievable when the Beebes got home that night.

"The neighbors had decorated the house," Diana said. "They had it all done up, and a sign across the garage that said, 'It's Beebe again,' like the announcers had said on Monday Night Football. It was special."

So special that Don and Diana, alone with his agents, Bob and Lynn LaMonte, who were in town, stayed up that night and watched the entire game again.

There was still a lot of football left, but the Packers enjoyed the high from stepping up one more rung on the ladder.

1996 was really a special year for the Beebes. MaKayla, born November 8, 1996, celebrates her first birthday.

21

SHE'S HAVING A BABY

The season had finally taken a turn distinctly in Beebe's direction. After the Monday night game with the 49ers on October 14, in which Beebe caught 11 passes for 220 yards as Green Bay won, it appeared Beebe was headed for an even bigger role. With injuries to starting wideout Robert Brooks and starting flanker Antonio Freeman, Beebe was being counted on more than ever by the Packers.

And at home, too. Diana was pregnant with the Beebes' third child. She was due the weekend of the Kansas City game.

The Packers needed a receiver, but football simply wouldn't come before faith or family for Beebe. Not only did the experience bring his family closer together, it brought him to hold Packers coach Mike Holmgren in an even higher regard. Equal parts motivator, strategist, organizer and family man, Holmgren assumed a bigger role in Beebe's life than Don ever thought was possible.

After a Diana's appointment Tuesday with her doctor, Beebe went to Holmgren's office on Wednesday morning, four days before the game with Kansas City. At that time, Beebe had become the Packers No. 1 receiver.

"Coach," Beebe told Holmgren, "I don't think my wife is going to make it through the week. We went to the doctor, and he said she's going to have the baby before the end of the week. Coach, if it comes down to being there for the birth of my child or playing, I'll be there for the birth of my child."

Holmgren could've handled it any number of ways.

"Don, I understand," Holmgren said. "I understand that. I respect that, and I completely agree with you. But is there something we can do? Something we can work out so we can have the child safely and still have you at the game? Because, obviously, we need you. But you are 100 percent right, the baby and the family come first. Without question, I want you to be there for the birth of your child."

At that point, Beebe was so thrilled with Holmgren's support that Beebe decided he'd see what he could do.

"I'll do everything under my power to be there at the game," Beebe said.

As soon as Beebe left Holmgren's office, the coach called Diana.

"Mrs. Beebe," he said. "This is Mike Holmgren, how are you doing?"

Diana had never talked to the coach before, and was

surprised by the call.

"Hi, coach," she said. "Fine. How are you?"

"I just talked to Don," Holmgren said. "Is there any-thing we can do to have the baby, and he could be at the game and everything could be all right?"

Diana was a little surprised. Don had insisted on being there for the birth. Football was going so well for the first time in several years. Diana, always Don's biggest sup-porter, did not feel he had to be there for the birth; she wanted him to get all he could out of the season and help the Packers because he was enjoying football more than he had since his days with the Buffalo Bills.

"Coach, he can be there for the game," Diana said. "He's been there for a C-section; he's been there for a natural birth. He doesn't need to be there this time."

Diana heard Holmgren chuckle.

"I appreciate that, Mrs. Beebe," Holmgren said. "But I still want to make sure Don is there. Can I have your doctor's name and number?"

Diana said sure, and gave him the number. Don got called back to talk to Holmgren.

"You know what, Don? Besides my wife, your wife is the greatest woman I ever met," Holmgren said. "She's unbelievable!"

Don didn't know what was going on, or that Holmgren had called Diana and her doctor.

"Don, I just want to let you know that I think we have everything worked out," Holmgren said. "The doctor said they can induce the labor, and everything will be fine. Diana will be healthy, and there's no risk to the baby."

Like X's and O's on a chalkboard, Holmgren's plan
worked to perfection. MaKayla Nicole Beebe brought her
8-pound, 2-ounce frame into the world Friday morning,
after doctors broke Diana's water late Thursday night.

"We went in Thursday night and had the baby Friday
morning," Don said. "And made the trip on Saturday to
Kansas City. I even made practice both days. But I didn't
sleep at all Thursday night."

Don's respect and affection for Holmgren grew as well.

"The point is that Mike was willing to sacrifice and
make sure family comes first," Don said. "That's just the
kind of guy Mike is. What Mike possesses, that a lot of guys
don't, is his rare combination of demanding respect and
demanding the best out of you, like a Mike Ditka or Bill
Parcells. But away from the field, he's your best friend. He
has that rare combination. He's a dominant figure on the
field, but off the field, you can approach him about anything and relate to him."

The scenario became sort of funny in Green Bay as the
story broke in the media. Not long before, a Houston player
had been fined for missing a game to see his child born. But
the Packers, a family sort of organization from top to
bottom—the team is owned publicly—apparently don't do
business that way. But the local media wanted to keep tabs
on the human interest story as it developed—every step of
the way.

"The hospital did a good job of keeping most of the
phone calls and visitors away," Don said. "But Diana was
in hard labor and the phone rings in the room. It's a
reporter, who says, 'Did you have the baby yet?' I said,

'Please, we're in labor, please don't call again.' I turn on the news that night, and they're showing the window of Diana's room in the hospital from the outside. The reporter said, 'This is the room where Mrs. Diana Beebe just had her and Don's baby, named MaKayla Nicole.'"

"It was crazy," Don said. "But it was also fun. The people in Green Bay were absolutely wonderful."

"This," Diana said, "will be something that MaKayla will get a big kick out of when she's older."

A few weeks before her first birthday MaKayla tried to impersonate a bag of leaves.

"The deepest and most talented receiving crew I've ever seen." Left to right: Antonio Freeman, Bill Schroeder, Robert Brooks, Terry Mickens, Don Beebe, Derrick Mayes, Desmond Howard, Andre Rison, and Eric Matthews. At the top, the leader of the pack, receivers coach Gil Haskell.

22

STRUGGLES, THEN THE PUSH
FOR HOME FIELD
ADVANTAGE

Packers 13, Buccaneers 7 (Oct. 27): Kind of a ho-hum game for Green Bay, which was as good as it needed to be and little else. Although the Packers did dominate Tampa Bay statistically, getting 24 first downs to only 14 for the Bucs, gaining more than 100 yards more of total offense than the Bucs (298 to 196) and rushing for 129 yards while holding the Bucs to only 57.

Brett Favre keyed the win, completing 19-of-31 passes for 178 yards. Desmond Howard led a balanced receiving corps. with five catches for 30 yards while tight end Mark Chmura caught three passes for a team-high 59 yards.

Beebe caught three balls for 23 yards.

"After you come off a big win like we did on Monday night—which was one of the bigger wins in Packer history, to tell you the truth—you do kind of settle into a lull," Beebe said. "We were kind of flat, we didn't play a great game. But our defense kept us in it. Great teams find a way to win. We were able to do that."

Packers 28, Lions 18 (Nov. 3): The Packers closed out their three-game homestand with a big win over Detroit, giving Green Bay a five-game winning streak, their longest since a six-game winning streak in 1982.

In running their record to 8-1, the Packers were scored upon first for the first time all season. The Lions had a 10-7 in the second quarter before the Packers answered with 21 consecutive points, and added another after a Detroit score. Favre threw a pair of touchdowns to Terry Mickens, and one each to Dorsey Levens and Beebe. The one to Beebe was by far the longest, a 65-yarder that put Green Bay up, 28-10.

"This is one of the most memorable games for me," Beebe said. "I get a lot of people, wherever I go, who talk about that Detroit game, and the San Francisco game, too. Because against Detroit, I got hit really hard twice—once at the one-yard line and once head to head with Bennie Blades. A couple series later though, I caught the 65-yard touchdown. People have told me they thought that was pretty cool. I didn't think anything of it. I was just doing my job."

Mickens, making his first NFL start, led the Packers with seven catches for 52 yards and two touchdowns. In the yardage department, Beebe led the way, getting 106 yards out of his four receptions, including the long TD catch. Favre hit on 24 of 35 passes for 281 yards. Edgar Bennett rushed 17 times for 68 yards and became just the eighth Packer to rush for 3,000 yards in his career.

Chiefs 27, Green Bay 20 (Nov. 10): The final three-game road trip of the season did not end up being bountiful for Green Bay. A 17-point second quarter by Kansas City, keyed by quarterback Steve Bono, was too much for Green Bay to overcome, although Favre did try, with a 25-yard touchdown pass to Beebe and a six-yarder to Derrick Mayes in the fourth quarter as the Packers scored the final 14 points to make a 27-6 game look much closer by the game's end.

"We knew going into the next three road games that this would be the toughest part of the year," Beebe said. "We had lost a few players, Robert (Brooks), Antonio (Freeman), and now Mark Chmura was hurt. To go into Kansas City, one of the toughest places to play, was a tough task. My days in Buffalo, when we played in Kansas City—and keep in mind, these are the years we went to the Super Bowl— they'd hand our lunch to us. It's just a tough place to play."

Statistically, the Packers were fine, with 24 first downs to 19 for Kansas City. The Chiefs had 383 yards of total offense to 364 for Green Bay. But the Chiefs did the job on the ground, rushing for 182 yards, while Green Bay could muster only 75 yards rushing. That meant the Packers had to rely on the pass, and Favre threw 47 passes, completing 27 and getting picked off only once. Beebe had three catches for 52 yards.

Cowboys 21, Packers 6 (Nov. 18): Host Dallas wasn't overpowering offensively, gaining only one more first down than Green Bay. But while the Cowboys didn't get into the end zone the whole game, they used their 309 yards of total offense to set up kicker Chris Boniol for seven field goals.

"It goes without saying that we wanted to win this game," Beebe said. "We wanted to win this game as badly as any other game. Then, we go in there and play awful. We didn't play flat. We just didn't play well. It got a little ugly. That was the toughest loss we faced all year."

Favre didn't surrender an interception and completed 21-of-37 passes for 194 yards, while Dallas quarterback Troy Aikman was better, hitting on 24-of-35 throws, with no interceptions, for 206 yards. Dallas running back Emmitt Smith had 76 yards—more than the combined total for Green Bay's top two backs, Edgar Bennett and Dorsey Levens , who had 48 yards and 26, respectively.

Beebe had one catch for 10 yards.

Packers 24, Rams 9 (Nov. 24): The last game of the season's final three-game road trip ended on a positive note as St. Louis fell meekly.

After a sluggish start that saw Green Bay fall behind 9-0 as time wound down in the first half, Green Bay had to punt for a "free kick" after the Rams recorded a safety. It started slipping from there for the Rams when Mike Prior got the Packers the ball at the St. Louis 37-yard line on the free kick. However, Green Bay did not turn that into any points. Doug Evans triggered a game-saving rally for the

Packers when he intercepted a Tony Banks pass on the second play of the third quarter and raced 32 yards for a touchdown to tie the game.

"Doug Evans made the play of the year," Beebe said. "That was the springboard to the rest of the season."

Chris Jacke's extra point put the Packers ahead for good. Favre hit for two more touchdown passes and became only the second quarterback in NFL history to throw 30 or more touchdown passes in three different seasons.

Recently acquired Andre Rison, who was drafted the same year as Beebe, made a big impression, leading the team with five catches for 44 yards.

"As much as people said Andre wouldn't fit in because of his dealings with other teams, I think he got a bad rap," Beebe said. "Andre's just a tough, competitive person. He was always on losing teams, and he just spoke his mind. He fit right in with the Green Bay guys. I knew him from years past. When I first saw him in Green Bay, I reminded him that we were the only two wide receivers left in the NFL from the 1989 draft. We first met at the NFL Combine in 1989. We hit it off right away. We had a great relationship."

Beebe again led the team in receiving yards, with 46 on four receptions.

"We felt going into St. Louis that it was a must win," Beebe said. "We had to win this game to save our season. We lose this game, it's three in a row, and our backs are to the wall. We still would make the Playoffs, but to get home field, we had to have it. It was a tough game. But we fought and fought and really showed our character."

Packers 28, Bears 17 (Dec. 1): The Packers assured themselves of a playoff berth, coupled with their win over Chicago and the Eagles' eventual loss four days later to Indianapolis.

Green Bay's first three touchdowns came on a pass, a return, and a run. Favre hit Keith Jackson for a 19-yard touchdown to tie the score at 7-7 at the half. Howard put Green Bay ahead for good with a 75-yard punt return in the third quarter. Levens and Favre added touchdown runs of 10 and one yards, respectively, in the fourth quarter.

Freeman had no touchdowns but still a big day, with 10 catches for 156 yards. Favre was an efficient 19-of-27 for 231 yards. Beebe caught two passes for 18 yards against the team he grew up rooting for.

"Mike (Holmgren) has found a way to have a great record against the Chicago Bears," Beebe said. "When they came up to Lambeau, special teams really handled the game. The defense shut them down, and we played well enough to win on offense."

Packers 41, Broncos 6 (Dec. 8): The Packers clinched their second consecutive NFC Central Division title with a 41-6 victory over Denver. Green Bay's record improved to 11-3, matching the entire win total for 1996.

"That was a key matchup of the year," Beebe said. "It hurt not having John Elway in there because you want to have John and Brett, the two MVP quarterbacks in there. It was the two best teams in the NFC and AFC. We just handled them."

The victory also marked the seventh time in team history that Green Bay had won 11 or more games. Leading by just a touchdown, 13-6, early in the second half, Favre took over in the third quarter when he hit Freeman with a pair of touchdown passes, one from 51 yards out and the other from 25. Favre also hit Keith Jackson for a one-yard touchdown. Freeman ended up with three touchdowns catches among his nine receptions for 175 yards.

"Antonio just went off in that game," Beebe said. "That game right there set Antonio apart, that he was becoming a big-time receiver. It opened some eyes around the league."

Beebe ended the scoring when he recovered a Travis Jervey fumble in the end zone.

For the fifth time of the season, Favre threw four touchown passes, tying him with Dan Marino for the second most such performances in a single season. Favre completed 20 of 38 passes for 280 yards. Levens helped the Packers with 86 yards on 14 carries. With John Elway on the bench, Denver's offense was far from being a mile high. Backup quarterback Bill Musgrave and the Broncos were held to 176 total offensive yards and no touchdowns, marking the fourth time that season the Packer defense refused to yield a touchdown.

Packers 31, Lions 3 (Dec. 15): The win over Detroit clinched a first-round bye for the playoffs. The game was closer than the score, at least through the first three quarters and especially the first half.

Beebe led all Green Bay receivers with 79 yards on four catches.

"I was fortunate to have a couple of big plays to help the team win," Beebe said. "It's tough, again, playing in a dome. It's always tough facing a guy the caliber of Barry Sanders. We actually handled them quite well."

All Green Bay put on the scoreboard in the first quarter was a 20-yard field goal by Jacke. The offense did not score a touchdown in the opening half, but Desmond Howard returned a punt 92 yards to put Green Bay up, 10-0 at the half.

"Desmond set the tone early in the game," Beebe said.

Favre added a one-yard run in the third quarter, and Green Bay scored twice more in the final quarter, including a 27-yard pass from Favre to Freeman. With Green Bay's defense yielding only 265 yards of total offense (to 336 for the Packers), the offense didn't have to do much. Favre still threw for 240 yards, completing 16 of 25 passes.

Packers 38, Vikings 10 (Dec. 22): This game ended up being big because it guaranteed the Packers would not have to leave Lambeau Field in the post-season, clinching home field throughout the playoffs.

"This was a big game for us because they beat us up there and we weren't going to have them beat us twice," Beebe said. "Mike (Holmgren) stressed that no one was going to beat us at Lambeau Field. That was a big issue for us. We played a good game. The weather wasn't that good, but we played well."

Tied at 10-10 at halftime, the Packers went out and scored 21 unanswered points in the second half, coming on three successive drives. Favre threw three touchdown passes, to three different receivers. He hit Levens on a 13-yard, Rison for 22 yards and a score, and Keith Jackson with a 23-yard scoring strike. The offense rolled up a season-high 440 yards. The running game had its best performance, with 233 yards on 41 carries, led by Bennett, who had 109 yards on 18 carries. That was the Packers only 100-yard individual rushing effort of the season, and the game itself produced the Packers lone 200-plus yard ground attack of the season.

Favre finished the regular season with 39 touchdowns, becoming only the third Packer and the 10th player in NFL history to lead the league in touchdown passes for two consecutive seasons.

Just showing off. Left to right, Kent Johnson (strength coach), Frank Winters, Mark Chmura, Brett Favre, and Don show off their Super Bowl rings at the ring ceremony.

With a microphone in his hand, Don screams: "REPEAT!
REPEAT!" at the 60,000 fans gathered in Lambeau Field at
the "Return to Title Town Super Bowl Parade and Party."

23

THE ROAD
TO THE SUPER BOWL
GOES THROUGH TITLETOWN

Packers 35, 49ers 14 (Jan. 4): With home field advantage firmly in tow, the Packers had a bye week before starting the Playoffs. All rested and healed, Green Bay put a second hurt on San Francisco.

Some "experts" wondered whether Green Bay could beat the 49ers again, after the Packers stopped San Francisco, 23-20, in overtime during the regular season.

"We were fortunate to have home field advantage," Beebe said. "But in comes the best team in the 1980s, and conceivably, the '90s. We were definitely confident we were going to win. With the Playoffs in Lambeau, we thought we'd win it all."

Any questions were answered quickly as the Packers advanced to the NFC Championship with a 35-14 dismantling of the Niners on a soggy field at rainy Lambeau Field.

"That weather was the worst I ever played in," said Beebe, who caught one pass for two yards as Green Bay turned to its running game for 139 yards, while passing for 71. San Francisco was just the opposite, watching the Packers shut down its running game for only 68 yards, while passing for 128.

"We could get no footing on that field," Beebe said. "The ball was slipping around like it was in a pigsty. Because of that game alone, the Packers and the NFL changed Lambeau Field's grass to where it can hold 15 inches of rain per hour."

Regardless, the frozen tundra on that day was a fitting resting spot for San Francisco's season. And almost no one in Green Bay missed it as a record crowd of 60,787 braved the weather, with only three no-shows.

Desmond Howard helped stake Green Bay to an early 14-0 lead. He returned the first punt of the game 71 yards for a touchdown. He followed that by returning the next punt to the San Francisco seven-yard line, setting up a four-yard pass from Brett Favre to Andre Rison two plays later.

"Desmond set the tone for us with those two great returns," Beebe said. "Those were just huge, and they put us up, 14-0."

The Packers expanded the margin to 21-0 in the second

quarter when Craig Newsome intercepted an Elvis Grbac pass to give Green Bay the ball at the San Francisco 15. Three plays later, Edgar Bennett dug his way into the end zone from two yards out.

The game was firmly in Green Bay's hands—or so it seemed until a pair of turnovers by the Packers led to two 49ers touchdowns, closing Green Bay's lead to seven, 21-14, in the third quarter. But the Packers followed the Niners' second touchdown with another score of their own. The drive went 72 yards in 12 plays, and was capped with a highlight when Antonio Freeman made a heads up play and recovered a fumble by Bennett in the soggy end zone, putting Green Bay back up by two TDs, 28-14.

The Pack added an insurance score when Mike Prior forced a fumble at the San Francisco 32-yard line that was recovered by Chris Hayes. Six plays later, Bennett ran in around the right side for a touchdown and the deciding margin.

"Obviously, the Playoffs are a do-or-die situation," Beebe said. "You win, you keep playing. You lose, you go home."

NFC Championship: Packers 30, Panthers 13 (Jan. 12): The Packers broke in their new turf by breaking the heart of Carolina fans, ending the two-year-old expansion franchise's dreams of a quick trip to the Super Bowl.

"Actually, I was a little surprised the way we handled them," Beebe said. "I felt like our defense in Lambeau Field, in cold weather, would dominate their offense. I thought their defense would give us a lot of trouble with zone blitzes—the outcome was very surprising to me."

It also marked an opportunity for Beebe to face the team that had cut him at the end of the 1995 season.

"As far as revenge factor, I had nothing," said Beebe, who played one year for the Panthers before signing with the Packers. "To tell you the truth, I had all the admiration in the world for the Panthers. For that time frame, to have Dom Capers to take them to a championship game in just their second season is one of the most remarkable things in NFL history. I was proud of them, I had friends on that team. But don't get me wrong, I wanted to win."

That part was almost too easy. Beebe caught one pass for 29 yards and running back Dorsey Levens was all over the field, catching five passes for 117 yards and rushing 10 times for 88 yards. Levens was hot on a day when the wind chill brought the temperature down from 3 degrees to as low as minus-23 during the game.

"That game right there," Beebe said, "put Dorsey Levens on the map to stardom."

The new turf, which cost $150,000, held up fine. The same could not be said for the Panthers. Carolina started out strong, intercepting Favre and then scoring for a quick 7-0 lead. But Favre got it back in a hurry, hitting Levens on the first play of the second quarter with a 29-yard touchdown pass. Another Green Bay fumble set up a Panthers field goal, and gave Carolina a 10-7 lead. Favre answered with a 71-yard, 15-play drive, finishing it off with a six-yard scoring strike to Freeman with two minutes left in the half. Green Bay cornerback Tyrone Williams intercepted a Carolina pass on the first play following the kickoff, and the Packers went for the jugular. Favre hit Rison for 23 yards and Freeman for 25 to set up a 31-yard field goal by Chris Jacke, which pushed Green Bay's lead to 17-10 at halftime.

Packer fans had to worry more about staying warm than about their team in the second half. Green Bay dominated, scoring on its first possession of the half and never looking back. Favre was solid, completing 19-of-29 passes for 292 yards and two touchdowns. The defense was also outstanding, holding the Panthers to 45 yards rushing.

Super Bowl XXXI: Packers 35, Patriots 21 (Jan. 26): Good things come to good people who wait, and after 29 years, the Lombardi Trophy returned to the home of its namesake.

Teammates asked Beebe what to expect in New Orleans as far as the atmosphere.

"We leaned on Don during the week leading up to the Super Bowl," said teammate Shannon Clavelle. "He had been to four, and most of us had never been to even one."

Beebe and backup quarterback Jim McMahon were the only Packers with Super Bowl experience.

"It was interesting," said Packer teammate Reggie White. "Because on the one hand, you had Don Beebe. On the other, you had Jim McMahon, who is a great leader, but not really like Don. But Jim is misunderstood, people who really know him really like him. And I still hope and believe that we (Christians) will get Jim one of these days."

Surprise AFC representative New England was little match for Green Bay as the game unfolded.

However, early, the game was close. After holding New England scoreless on its first series, the Packers struck on just their second play of the game. Favre changed the play at the line of scrimmage when he read a blitz, and threw a 54-yard touchdown strike to Andre Rison. Two plays later, Patriots quarterback Drew Bledsoe was picked off by Doug Evans, which lead to a field goal by Green Bay.

New England became the Minutemen in the flesh, driving 79 yards in six plays to get within a field goal. But the Patriots had that and more up their sleeve, pulling ahead, 14-10, on a four play, 57-yard drive with 2:33 left in the first quarter.

"In Super Bowl XXXI, we (Green Bay) were beating the Patriots, 10-0," Beebe recalls. "All of a sudden, we face adversity. New England scored two touchdowns, and it was 14-10. We stood there and said, 'We're going to do what we've done all year, and we're going to beat these guys down."

Green Bay was unfazed. Favre hit Freeman with an 81-yard touchdown pass, the longest play from scrimmage in Super Bowl history. The Packers added a field goal and two-yard touchdown run by Favre to go ahead, 27-14 at the half.

New England started a final rally in the third quarter when Curtis Martin scored on an 18-yard touchdown run, slicing the Packers' lead to six, 27-21. But on the next play, the kickoff, Desmond Howard ensured another title for Titletown when he returned the kickoff 99 yards and a score, setting a Super Bowl record. Fare hit tight end Mark Chmura with the two-point conversion pass to put the Packers back up by 14, 35-21. A scoreless four quarter left that as the final margin. Howard was incredible, becoming the first-ever special teams player to earn Super Bowl Most Valuable Player honors, returning four kickoffs for 154 yards and six punts for 90 yards. The Packers defense, led by Reggie White's Super Bowl record three sacks, held the Patriots to only 43 yards rushing.

"The game itself was great," Beebe said. "It would've been great to catch a ball or be more involved. But my main objective was to win it, to get the world championship ring. I was very satisfied."

Friends from his football days in Buffalo also smiled.

"Thank goodness for him, he finally got his ring," Nicolau said. "I was watching him, and I was just delighted."

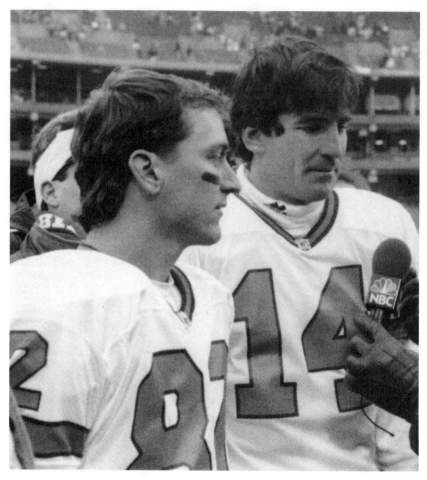

Don and his best friend Frank Reich. While playing for the
Buffalo Bills, Don met quarterback Frank Reich, and a life-
time friendship resulted.

24

A FRIENDSHIP FOREVER

When Don and his best friend, Frank Reich, get together, it's almost like they are high schoolers.

"Don has one of the best senses of humor you'd ever want to be around," Reich said. "He's extremely funny. Whenever we go out, whether just the two of us or with our wives, people look at us like we've had too much to drink—only none of us drink. We just have a very good time together. And our wives are close as well. We enjoy each other's company."

The foundation of their friendship is their faith.

"The thing that has bonded us is our love for the Lord," Reich said. "We grow in fellowship in the word of God. I believe one of the gifts God has given Don is great faith. As a result, Don has a lot of peace about him, all the positive characteristics of a person—the never-say-die attitude and the kind of things that are the result of Don being grounded in his faith. That is the root of everything good."

The pair got close after Beebe's rookie year during a three-hour round-trip in a car to a speaking engagement.

"He told me his whole story, how he got to the NFL, and I had never heard it before," Reich said. "It was so moving, and I had so much respect for what he had gone through to get to the NFL. Looking back, that's where this friendship started."

Reich, who ended up, like Beebe, leaving Buffalo for Carolina that year, said Beebe underestimates his contributions in Buffalo.

"There's no doubt Don was a huge part of the legacy in Buffalo," Reich said. "He definitely has his part in Buffalo history, for a number of reasons. First, he was part of the Super Bowl runs. He has the record for most touchdown catches in a game, and he had some really big plays. Secondly, the people in the Buffalo community know what kind of person Don is."

Beebe hosts a golf tournament each summer in Chadron to benefit Chadron State College. Reich is now a regular participant.

"He showed me the field at the college, and it was like, 'Wow!' I mean, it was nice, but not very big at all," Reich said. "It's hard to believe that was part of his route to the NFL. But then you go around the town of Chadron itself, and the place is just something else. You go out there and just fall in love with it. The people are just great, as friendly as they come. And it was neat to see the impact that Don has had on the town, and the impact the town has had on

Don. Chadron is a part of who Don is."

Along with Chadron State football coach Brad Smith and Bills' All-Pro Steve Tasker, Beebe and Reich went up the road less than an hour to Hot Springs, South Dakota, for dinner one night.

"The guys walk in and no one knows who they are," Smith recalls with a smile. "I mean, everyone out this way says, 'Hi,' to everyone, whether they know you or not. But we sit down in a booth to eat, and no one bothers the guys. Frank was like, 'Man, I could get used to this.'"

On the golf course, Beebe rules.

"Really, a lot of the fun times have come when we're out golfing," Reich said. "And yes, as Don will tell you, he is a better golfer than I am. There was a day when that was not true. But now, it is true. You know, Don played college basketball (at Aurora College). Ask Don who won when we played one-on-one."

Well?

"Come on, Frank is six-foot-four," Beebe says wryly. "Two of three, and yes, he won two, but it did go three."

The pair leaned on each other during each of Buffalo's four Super Bowl defeats as well.

"Don and I would always talk about it from a spiritual standpoint: What is God trying to teach us?" Reich said. "You'd think after one, two or three, that you have to win one. When that never happened, we'd be flying home on the plane, wondering, 'What can we learn out of this?' knowing the full well that we'd done everything in our power to win. Having the outcome the way it was each time, there was constantly that learning.

"I believe ultimately, you turn a defeat into a victory by maturing as a person and a football player," Reich said. "Just because the game was a loss, it doesn't have to have a lingering effect. After a tough loss, the way to deal with it is make it a positive."

Reich, not a regular viewer of Monday Night Football, watched the game between the 49ers and Packers in 1996 to see if Beebe was in the lineup.

"I rarely watch Monday Night Football just because during the season, I'm trying to get some rest," Reich said. "That particular night, I turned it on and thought I'd watch a quarter. I started watching to see what Don's doing. He starts catching everything, and I told my wife, 'I'm not going to bed now!' Literally and truthfully, I've never had so much fun watching a football game. Now, I finally know how my family feels when they watch me play. I was so happy for him and his family."

Knowing Beebe as well as he does, Reich wasn't surprised at the big game Beebe came up with in front of the country on a Monday Night Football telecast against one of the great teams of the past decade.

"Don's always had a knack for making big plays," Reich said. "His whole career, he's done that. Don's always been the one to come up big in important games."

Beebe, Reich, and Steve Tasker had dinner two nights before the Packers won the Super Bowl.

"It ended up that I couldn't stay for the game, so I had to watch it on television," said Reich who signed on with the Jets after Carolina and then ended up in Detroit for the 1997 season. "It was a great thrill to see Don and the

Packers win. I truly felt a sense of accomplishment myself, just watching Don. The Super Bowl isn't the end for all the world, but for football, it is the ultimate goal. I was excited to see my best friend in that position, for him to experience a championship. Steve and I knew how tough it was to get there. We know how hard the work is."

So does Don.

Don's good friend Jim Kelly with Chad and Amanda at
Jeff Still's Camp of Dreams.

Don and some close friends at his golf tournament in
Chadron. Left to right: Ben Smith, Don, Steve Tasker, Brad
Smith, and Frank Reich.

25

BUFFALO BUDDIES: KELLY AND TASKER

Leaving Buffalo for Carolina, and ultimately, Green Bay was hard on Beebe for a number of reasons. In addition to being close to Frank Reich and the coaching staff, Beebe had developed friendships with Jim Kelly and Steve Tasker.

Kelly, a certain Hall of Famer who quarterbacked the Bills to four Super Bowl appearances, said Beebe had a well-deserved reputation as a player who always went 100 percent, so much so that it occasionally drew the wrath of teammates in practice. At the same time, Kelly said Beebe was all "Prairie Boy" when he showed up for functions off the field in Buffalo, especially at first.

"Ask Don about the first time he showed up for a team

function—I think it was a dinner," Kelly said, laughing. "He shows up in a half-leisure suit that ends at the waist. He thinks it looks cool, which shows how much he knew about clothes. I mean, people there who didn't know him thought he was a waiter. My teammates and I were like, 'Don, get me a glass of water,' or, 'We need a soda here.'

"He got abused so bad that it was hysterical," Kelly said. "Everybody made so much fun of him. He didn't get it. He came up and asked, 'Why is everyone laughing? Why are people asking me for a glass of water?' And this thing was at least 90-percent polyester—wait, make that 100-percent polyester. But we all knew that Don was never one to reach too deep into his pocket."

"What he looked like was a bad maitre d'," Tasker said, "at a really bad restaurant."

So, Don, what about that suit?

"Oh, man, I can't believe Jim mentioned that," Beebe answered, embarrassed. "It was a kickoff luncheon for the team, and I was a rookie. I had this black jacket. I thought that suit was bad to the bone when I bought it —really cool. Everyone had busted out their best suit for that dinner. I thought mine was the best suit known to mankind. I guess the coat was kind of short, now that I think about it. Yeah, sort of maybe like a waiter, I guess."

Tasker was among a group of players who dined with Beebe, then a rookie, during a preseason trip to play the Packers in Green Bay.

"We got up and stuck him with a $260 check for dinner," Tasker said with a smile. "That was a rite of passage for rookies. But Don calls us back, and really lays a big guilt trip on us. 'You guys do this to me, and I'm new here, I have no money, I have a lot of bills. How can you do this?' We all felt so guilty because that had never happened before—that's just something you do to rookies each year, especially a top draft pick. We all started reaching into our pockets because we felt so bad—you have to understand, he just went on and on and on. Then after we had our wallets out, Don pops up and pays the bill on his own—so he got us pretty good with the guilt trip. In fact, whenever Don and Frank and I go out to eat, we still hear about it."

Kelly said Beebe was a team player from start to finish. "He never wanted to show anyone up—he wasn't the kind to brag. He was just such a competitor. More than that, he was a good teammate, a good friend and a great family man. Everyone around him knew it."

While injuries slowed Beebe at various times, Kelly said Beebe played with no fear. "More than anything, Don was the kind of player who wanted to be on the field all the time," Kelly said. "A lot of times I felt bad when I led him too much across the middle, and he'd get hit pretty hard or knocked on his butt. But we joked about it. He always made those of us around him feel better. There's no doubt that Don worked his butt off. It wasn't like anything was ever given to him. One thing about Don, he has the heart of a giant. He wanted to be in there, putting his body on the line. I am honored to say I played with Don Beebe. He was a huge part of what we did in Buffalo, and also putting in the no-huddle offense. And what I really remember when I think back to those times with Don and those guys is this: We had an awful lot of fun."

What Beebe didn't do also caught Kelly's attention.

"If he didn't catch any passes, he never complained," Kelly said. "I know a lot of players who complain if they don't have a lot of passes thrown their way. But Don was 100 percent a team player."

Those big hits to which Kelly referred made Beebe the brunt of a lot of joking in Buffalo's film room.

"I tease Don a lot," Tasker said. "I kid him about how a lot of people know him because he's a poster boy for taking a big shot—a huge hit. I tell him to forget all that speed, the catch and the yardage—he's famous because he's on every highlight film for landing on his head or taking a huge hit."

Teasing aside, Tasker said he has always been amazed at Beebe's resiliency. "He broke his leg his second year in Buffalo, and then the next year he broke his collarbone," Tasker said. "So the year after that, we were setting goals. I told him not to set any goals for catches and yards, but to make his goal to not break a bone."

When Beebe asked Kelly to come to Illinois during the spring of 1997 for a football camp to benefit Jeff Still's children (Still, a close friend of Beebe's, was killed by a drunk driver), Kelly said he'd be there, despite a hectic schedule arranged long in advance.

"Don was one of the my closest friends—a great guy, a family man," Kelly said. "Number one, Don is a good friend. He told me about the situation where his friend had been killed. I said, 'Don, you've always been there for me and done whatever I asked.' So I said, 'I'll be there for you.' It works both ways. If I ever have the opportunity again, I'll be there to help him. We continue to be the best of friends."

Tasker has gone to Chadron, Nebraska, several times for Beebe's annual benefit golf tournament for Chadron State College in the summer.

"The other players who go talk about what a small, remote town Chadron is," Tasker said. "But I came from a small town, so Chadron would've been a step up. I really enjoy going to Chadron. I like the people and the golf tournament. And it's always a good chance to see Don."

While Kelly's impressive credentials don't include a Super Bowl championship ring, he's well aware that Beebe has one. Beebe made sure Kelly knew when Beebe picked him up at the airport for the benefit football camp.

"Don showed up at the airport in flip-flop sandals, a tank top, and shorts," Kelly said. "But he's wearing this big ol' ring. He kept holding his hand up, rubbing his eye, and running his hand through his hair. I came down an escalator where he was waiting, and I was just laughing the whole way. He asked, 'Oh, did you see my Super Bowl ring?' I laughed. I said, 'I saw it from the top of the escalator.'"

Beebe, who doesn't drink alcohol, had made a deal with Kelly.

"I said, 'Don, if we win a Super Bowl, you have to sit down and have a beer with me,'" Kelly said. "Don said, 'Okay, Jim, if we win a Super Bowl, we'll do that.' Well, we didn't end up winning a Super Bowl together. So he goes to Green Bay, and of course, he gets the ring. So I asked him if he had a beer yet. He said, 'See that was the key to getting one of these rings. Brett Favre never asked me to have a beer with him.' Don has a great sense of humor, and that's something not a lot of people know about him."

Tasker, who dined with Beebe and Frank Reich before the Super Bowl, said he became a big Packer fan on Super Bowl Sunday.

"I couldn't have been happier for him. I was pulling for the Packers to win, just for Don," Tasker said. "There's a lot been said about the NFC beating the AFC, but even with all that stuff, I wanted Don to be on world championship team. He was here for all of our success, and then he got the ring—I couldn't have been happier. It's over said about a winner, that 'he deserved it.' But with Don, that really is the case. He's one of those people you meet who you will always root for."

Kelly also recalls Beebe as one of the fastest players in the league.

"I know Don is one of the top two fastest I ever threw the ball to," Kelly said. "When I was in the USFL, I threw to Ricky Sanders, and he was fast. Ricky and Don are definitely the two fastest I ever saw."

No matter how much time or distance lays between them, Kelly and Tasker said they always get smiles on their faces when they think about Beebe.

"There's no doubt that I'll remember Don Beebe as not only a great athlete," Kelly said, "but also as one of my dearest, closest friends."

"We'll probably never live near each other again because of how everything worked out with our careers," Tasker said. "But we'll be close friends forever."

26
BEING A ROLE MODEL

The Super Bowl win for Green Bay in the 1996 season gave Beebe not just a ring, but another opportunity.

"It is amazing how everything turned out," Beebe said. "I had the most catches in one game, and the longest kickoff return in the regular season. I was able to do a lot of things, and that was part of the Lord's plan for me. Because I'm at a level where enough people recognize me where I can get my witness out."

Beebe also knows that he's a role model.

"I know some athletes are not comfortable with that," Beebe said. "But I am. Still, the role model has to be in the family. My father is my role model. I am so proud of him and what he did for our family. He is my role model. It has to start with the Lord, and in the home. That's where it all started for me."

His close friends appreciate that.

"I realize I'm a role model, and Don knows he is, too," Packers' teammate Reggie White said. "Charles Barkley knows he's a role model, even though he says he's not. But get Barkley's point, the number one role model in a kid's life is the Mom and Dad. Don is the kind who is proud to be a role model. And his kids couldn't have a better role model than him."

Beebe's adherence to doing the right thing made teams proud in a day and age where professional athletes seem to all too often find themselves out of bounds when it comes to dealing with the law.

"Don always made my job five times easier," said Bills public relations director Scott Berchtold. "Don's such a classy guy, and he really enjoys any charitable effort. He carries himself with such dignity and class. When you have a guy like Don Beebe, you never have to worry about him getting in trouble or casting the team in a bad light."

No one from the Bills has bad memories from Beebe's time in Buffalo.

"Don sets an example that I'd like to see from everyone," said Bills general manager John Butler.

"He's a great guy, a model guy," said Nick Nicolau, who joined the San Diego Chargers for the 1997 season but coached Beebe in Buffalo. "He's a great family guy and a caring person. You had to feel he'd always be a professional with a capital 'P'."

Beebe carried himself the same way in Green Bay, setting an example not just for the young Packers' fans, but his teammates as well.

"He has a lot of determination to do the job," Packers quarterback Brett Favre said. "And it's the way he handles himself that says it all."

"Don is one of the leaders on the team," said Green Bay teammate Shannon Clavelle, a defensive tackle. "He's very humble, but very approachable."

"Don's not one of those rah-rah kind of players," said Steve Bono, who joined Green Bay in 1997 to be the backup to Favre. "He leads by example, who brings a lot of good qualities to the team. You get to know him and right away, you see that never-say-die attitude."

Beebe is a huge celebrity back in Chadron. He hasn't forgotten his roots there.

"Chadron and the people there are a big reason I'm where I am today," Beebe said. "Chadron is a huge part of who I am. I could never forget those people and the town."

Beebe still invites friends from Chadron to Green Bay. He plays golf with his former landlord, Bill Howard, from that year in the "mother-in-law" house in Chadron, in addition to the golf benefit he puts on annually for Chadron State College.

"You meet Beebs one time and you fall in love with him," Chadron State College football coach Brad Smith said. "His character, his humbleness, and his faith make him so special."

Beebe's ability to be a straight arrow in an era where so many professional, and even college, athletes are out of bounds lawfully makes it easy to be an agent.

"They don't get any better than Don and Diana Beebe," said Bob LaMonte of PSR, Inc., Beebe's agent. "He's a great player and a great person. He's a family man with high principles."

As his career winds down, Beebe is looking forward to more and more time with his wife, Diana, and his three children, Amanda, Chad, and MaKayla. Beebe explains how grateful he is for his family:

"The key is that Diana is my best friend. In any marriage if you don't get along and you aren't friends first, it would be very tough to have a good marriage," Beebe said. "I can share anything with her, and she can share anything with me. We don't hide anything from each other. When it's like that, you can trust each other.

"To tell you the truth, when I was in high school and going through college, all I really wanted was a good marriage and kids, raising kids, and just having as much fun as I can with my kids and watching them grow. That's really what I wanted more than anything. Obviously, football was a big aspiration for me. But first and foremost, if I had to give up one, without question I'd give up football—it wouldn't be a hard decision. I've been fortunate not just to be married to the best woman in the world, but to have three great kids. They're great kids, cute, beautiful, healthy, and a lot of fun. I can't ask for anything more.

"I've always said the greatest thing in this life is a good marriage. The worse thing in this world is a bad marriage. I mean, can you imagine coming home every day to a bad marriage? That would be miserable. God has blessed me and given me a lot of things. But the best gift He has given me is my family. The four of them are great."

Amanda at age 2. "She'll always be my little buddy."

Marv Levy. "A true gentleman and a man I will always, admire."

Extra Point

by
Marv Levy
Head Coach, Buffalo Bills

I have really good memories of Don. He gave every-thing he had all the time. He was a tremendous competitor. He was a perfect fit on the football field with the rest of the cast we had. He certainly complemented James Lofton, Andre Reed, and Pete Metzelaars. And of course, Jim Kelly and Thurman Thomas, the other skill position players. Don made a lot of big plays for us.

When Don broke his leg against Miami, he came back and was as fast as he was before. I think what he did there —not only did he show to the world what a fighting heart is about—he exhibited not only his fighting heart, but what the Buffalo Bills are about. No matter how bad the situation is, we don't give in.

He was a fine young man and a good citizen. He was

liked and respected by his teammates and the community
We put a lot of credence—when we pick a player—in the
quality of their character. He doesn't have to be a Sunday
school student—it's fine if he is—but just so long as he's a
good citizen who shows up for work everyday and
presents himself well off the field.

I don't know if we thought he'd be available when we
drafted him in the third round in 1989 with our first pick of
the Draft that year. But since he was a small college player
at Chadron State, you can't really be surprised to see him
still there in the third round.

I remember talking to Don on the phone on Draft day.
He was excited, and I could put myself in his shoes, joining
an NFL team, even though I didn't play in the NFL, after
the journey he took to get to Chadron.

The first time Don came to town, I was eating at a
restaurant and Don, his wife, and his agent came into the
same restaurant. Don really made a favorable impression,
just a wide-eyed kid with a great perspective.

I remember last year (1996), the game Don had against
the 49ers on Monday Night Football (Beebe had 11 catches
for 220 yards). I was kind of surprised. Don has overcome
a lot. He's not a big fella. He plays with great enthusiasm,
and he comes back from injuries with a great work ethic.

But consider what he has gone through. We didn't
know if he could hold up because of the degree he had
been injured, and we couldn't retain him because of the
salary cap. He goes to Carolina, but then they let him go.
From a distance, you think, "Yeah, his career is winding
down, and maybe it's over."

But Don Beebe has some special qualities. I was really happy for him. I have great regard for him, and I was glad to coach a young man like Don Beebe. By the time he left, it was almost like we were all family.

Postscript
LEADING
A SPIRIT-FILLED LIFE

by
Don Beebe

After reading my story, you can see where Jesus Christ's handprints are all over my life. The greatest gift the Lord has given me is my faith. That's not saying I haven't had my ups and downs, because I have.

I have made mistakes. But I've always tried to live a Spirit-filled life.

I knew when I went to Western Illinois the first time, in 1983, that I didn't feel right. I could tell that was not where the Lord wanted me to be at that time in my life. There are several times when there's no shadow of a doubt as to what you should do. There are other times when it's not clear, or you might have questions. But if you're doing God's will, you are headed in the right direction. The Holy Spirit will help us find the good when we make a bad decision, such as when we learn from our mistakes. You have to know that God is with you; He will get you through it, and give you the strength to do endure it.

When I went to Aurora College to play basketball—my first love when it comes to sports—I can't say if that was the Lord's will or not. But the Lord worked it out for me. And once again the key was that I prayed and learned from my time there.

When I was hanging siding, I had an urge to go back to school and play football. I wasn't sure where God wanted me to go to do that. I started praying, asking the Lord to open up some doors and show me what to do. Then, a week later, I got a call from Western Illinois, saying they wanted me to come back. That was the Lord's will. I was ready for college again at that time. When you're comfortable with something, you're deep in prayer and you feel comfortable, the Spirit is letting you know that this is what the Lord wants you to do. Of course, there are other ways He can let you know, too. It could be through His word or, in my case, He uses my best friend, my wife Diana, a lot.

There's no question that Chadron State was the Lord's will. I did not want to go out there at all. Diana and I had become engaged. The other college recruiting me, Illinois Benedictine, was perfect, and there were a lot of reasons to go there.

But I prayed, "Lord, I want to do your will. You know what it will take to get me into the NFL. If it means going to one of the most remote areas of the country to a college not many people have heard of, I will go. I will do what you want me to do." Even though I didn't want to do it, I felt comfortable with it. Through my conscience, my feelings and reading the Scripture, I knew that's where the Lord wanted me to be. Several times I read Proverbs 3:5-6 "Trust in the Lord with all your heart and lean not on your own understanding. In all your ways, acknowledge Him, and He will set your path straight."

That verse says it all: "Trust in the Lord with all your heart"—give it all to Him, don't leave any of it behind. Illinois Benedictine was the obvious choice, but it wasn't the Lord's way for me. I didn't do what I wanted to do, I did what the Lord wanted. When I made my choice, I woke up the next morning and felt great about it. I called Chadron State College football coach Brad Smith and said, "I don't know why, but I'm coming."

As I said in the book, we had $100 in our pocket. We had no idea where we were going to live. We just went on complete faith that God would take care of it all. People get worried doing things that take them out of their comfort zone. At times, you have to step out on faith and watch the Lord work. All of our needs, in a short period of time, were taken care of. As far as finances, sure, it was tough. But we learned a lot from that. We look back today at the lessons the Lord taught us from that.

Another reading from the Scripture that helped was Psalms 46:10. "Be still and know that I am God."

When I get confused and I'm stressed out and worried, I become still and say, "What am I doing here? I'm trying to do things on my own again." So I confess my sins to the Lord and give the control back to Him.

Buffalo wasn't my first choice when the NFL draft came around, but I really didn't have a first choice. Diana wanted to go somewhere warm. My thought at that time was, "Lord, you know my future better than I do. The right team will draft me."

Without a doubt in my mind, Buffalo was the right team for me. I could've gone to another team that wasn't very good. But on a winning team, everyone seems to become well known. That got my name out there and I was able to share my faith. The Lord was able to use my name as far as witnessing because of that situation—I was on a good team. That's not to say there aren't Christians on bad teams, because the Lord is using them in His way in those cases, too. God used me on the Buffalo Bills because He knew that would be the perfect situation.

Like I said in the book, when I left Buffalo, Carolina wasn't the place for me when it came to football. But the Lord had a plan for me, Frank Reich and Pete Metzalaars on the Carolina Panthers. That wasn't for football. I had to struggle and learn that. But now when I look back, I understand what the Lord was taking me through. I really matured as a Christian man.

I believe Green Bay was the other side of it, as it was with the Bills: I've still grown, but God has used me through football again. Because of the big games I had in 1996, and since we won the Super Bowl, I was able to share God's gospel through a lot of speaking engagements in the off-season. It wouldn't have been to the same magnitude had we not won the Super Bowl.

Of course, you learn through both winning and losing. As far as sharing your faith, people are more apt to listen to a winner. Because of the Super Bowl, people were able to listen to Eugene Robinson, Reggie White, Ken Ruettgers, Keith Jackson, myself and several others spread God's word.

You might make choices that are a little unclear, but you have to move forward.

I know that my faith in God is everything—putting Christ first in every aspect of my life. That doesn't mean only putting him first in my family, my career and then maybe not in finances and other things: You have to put Christ first in every aspect of your life, or it's hard for him to answer your prayers and lead you.

You have to give up everything to Him. There's nothing we're in control of, because if we are, that's like saying, "God is not in control. I can do it alone." That's not the way to lead a Spirit-filled life. When Christians stay in control of certain aspects of their life, they get unanswered prayer. God can't answer prayer when there's sin in your life. The sin I am talking about here is known sin, meaning when you know something is wrong, and you deliberately disobey God and do your own thing. There is also unknown sin, which are sins that we may be doing, but God has neither convicted nor revealed those to us yet. But you should pray for God to reveal all sin in your life (Psalms 139:23-24). And He will, in His perfect time. So back to my original thought, you have to get rid of all known sin in your life before God can answer prayer and work in and through you.

There are three types of people: The Natural person, who does not believe in God; The Spiritual Christian, who gives God everything. The third person is the Worldly Christian, who believes in Jesus Christ but wants to do his own will, not God's will. For the Natural person, God cannot hear his prayer, except one, the prayer to receive salvation.

The Spiritual Christian is living for the Lord and has confessed his sins. He is able to listen to the Lord and understand him. The Lord leads him, and the Spiritual Christian has his prayers heard. If you have sin in your life and are confessing it back to God, then you are maturing in this sort of lifestyle. Your prayers will be directed towards God's will. The material things of the world will be unimportant and will take care of themselves.

This is why I was able to make the right decisions; to go to Chadron State, to go back to Western Illinois, because I was doing the Lord's will for my life.

You can fall in and out of that. When I was younger, I let sin linger on for weeks and months. During that time I was doing my own thing, not the will of the Lord, because I hadn't confessed.

In making those tough decisions, I was able to get into prayer and let the Lord lead me. I was not leading myself. The Lord was leading me. The thing I'm learning is to continually, day in and day out, live the Spirit-filled life and know what the Lord wants from me. That's called maturing in your walk with the Lord.

I think the more you learn how to live a Spirit-filled life, the less you sin because the more you're filled with the Spirit daily. You know you can't do anything by yourself. Because you will fail, get stressed out, and be miserable. You'll know when there's sin in your life because the Holy Spirit convicts us.

As I stated, when I was younger and I would sin, I wouldn't confess right away. During that time, I was frustrated and stressed because I was doing things my way. The more I learned from the Lord, the more I confessed when sin came into my life. There are times when we don't know about sin in our life, but it's there. It is then that I pray, "Lord, if there's unconfessed sin in my life, if I've had anger toward a certain person or some kind of fear, I ask You, Lord, to bring it to me." And He will, through His word, prayer, or some other avenue.

For example, there were years when I had hidden anger toward a certain individual. I hid it, and we treated each other nicely. However, I still had it inside, even though I wouldn't show it. Then one day, I was doing a study on anger and fear, and, sure enough, the Lord brought it to me, because I had asked the Lord to bring it to me.

I prayed, "Lord, I don't want to be angry with this person. Help me love this person and share the fruits of the spirit with this person." As soon as I confessed it to the Lord, my attitude changed. And not only had my attitude changed, that person's attitude changed toward me. That's not to say that person and I became best friends, because we didn't. But ever since then, that relationship has changed and our relationship is better.

The key to leading a Spirit-filled life is to totally confess every sin that you know of to our Lord. Each person is different; they know what the sin is in their own lives, or their own hangups. You have to know what they are, confess them and get rid of them. Because you can't handle them.

For example, I said cuss words way too much in high school, and I confessed it to God. I said, "God, I cuss way too much and I want you to take it out of my life." I believed by faith, and to date, it no longer controls me. Now I still sin (Romans 3:23), but the key is to give up control. When you sin, confess it right away. Don't let it linger on in your life because sin can take away the fruits of the spirit that God has for us (Galatians 5:22-23). You can be anywhere during the course of your day and confess your sins to God. God is anxiously waiting to regain control of your life. So if you're living the Spirit-filled life, the Lord can answer your prayers and guide you. I like how they call it "Walking with the Spirit." You're doing the Lord's will, instead of your will.

You are being led by the Spirit. I don't want anyone to get this confused with someone who becomes a born-again Christian and says that they are "filled with the Spirit" because they are. We receive the Holy Spirit when we accept Jesus Christ.

Walking with the Spirit is when you have accepted Christ. From that point on, are you going to do what the Spirit wants you to do or what you want to do? You can fall out of that by doing your own will. But once you confess it and get rid of it, then you are leading the Spirit-filled life. It is not about how much of God we can get, but how much

God can get of us.

May God bless you in your Christian walk and your pursuit of the Spirit-filled life.

Index

PHOTO CREDITS

Don Beebe family collection: p. *xii, xiv*, 8, 9, 18, 19, 20, 21, 22, 23, 24, 25, 26, 27, 28, 32, 33, 34, 43, 48, 71, 72, 73, 97, 98, 107, 108, 122, 123, 140, 150, 157, 170 bottom, 176, 181, 182, 191, 192, 200, 206, 217

Jeff Still family collection: p. 7

The Wedding Gallery Ltd., Naperville, IL: 35, 81

Western Illinios University: p. 43

Buffalo Bills: p. 122, 138, 218

Bill Wippert: p. 124 bottom, 139

Jim Biever: p. 124 top, 158, 170 top, 222

Mike Groll: p. 141

ABOUT BOB SCHALLER

Born Robert Charles Schaller, Jr., on September 1, 1965 at Travis Air Force Base, California, Bob grew up to be a sportswriter. He earned a B.A. degree in Technical Journalism from Colorado State University in 1988, then joined the working press as an associate sports editor for the Antelope Valley (California) *Daily Press*. He became sports editor for the Scottsbluff (Nebraska) *Star-Herald* in 1991 and remained there until August 1997.

A man of no mean conviction Bob took a leap of faith and resigned his post with the newspaper to write *More Than A Ring* with Don Beebe because his employer wouldn't grant him a leave of absence to work on the project.

Bob was a Heisman Trophy voter at the *Star-Herald*, and also while there, he was named Nebraska sports columnist of the year by the Nebraska Press Association.

Bob has one son, Garrett Paul Schaller, born October 29, 1993, and he lives in Gering, Nebraska, just south of Scottsbluff.